BORN IN BETHLEHEM

H. W. VAN DER VAART SMIT

BORN IN BETHLEHEM

CHRISTMAS AS IT REALLY WAS

translated from the German

by

THOMAS R. MILLIGAN

HELICON

BALTIMORE — DUBLIN

Helicon Press, Inc.
1120 N. Calvert Street
Baltimore, Maryland, 21202

Helicon Limited
53 Capel Street
Dublin 8, Ireland

Library of Congress Catalog Card Number 63-19399

Translated from the German *Geboren zu Bethlehem*,
Patmos-Verlag, Düsseldorf, 1961.

Nihil Obstat: Carroll E. Satterfield
Censor Librorum

Imprimatur: ✠ Lawrence J. Shehan, D.D.
Archbishop of Baltimore
July 30, 1963

Second printing: April, 1964.

PRINTED IN THE REPUBLIC OF IRELAND
BY CAHILL & COMPANY LIMITED DUBLIN

CONTENTS

BORN IN BETHLEHEM

INTRODUCTION

AT CHRISTMAS time the green fir trees, the artificial snow and the Santa Clauses on the street corners evoke a romantic mood that draws the whole world under its spell, but which nonetheless stands in essential contradiction to Bethlehem and the birth of Jesus Christ. "Santa Claus" has as little to do with the infant Jesus as fir trees and snow have to do with the actual events in Bethlehem. Nordic and Christian elements undergo a strange and often garish blend beneath this romantic aura.

Yet in all this there is something worthwhile. At Christmas the world seems to pause for a moment in its frenetic pace, as if a traffic policeman had suddenly raised his hand and called a halt. For a time the world acts as if it liked to be soothed by this poetic calm. In the midst of its ornaments humanity seems to gaze at the image of Mary and her child as they illumine the world with a light that is not an everyday thing. A quiet homage to the event of Christmas is not absent here.

But can we be content with just this? I think not. The green enchantment of the Christmas season tends to thrust the real events of Christmas into the realm of the fabulous and unhistorical. In time the children no longer know whether Santa Claus is the Christ child or vice-versa, and in their psyches the romantic notions of Christmas toss about in gay confusion. We are slightly astonished to learn that even preachers of the Glad Tidings, and especially those men (and women) who are Christmas "narrators,"[1] ignore the historically attested facts and lose themselves in fairy tales. With their preference for the romantic trappings these people manifest a negligence of a very odd sort.

It has often been my experience that the cry, "Back to the historical sources" has been dismissed as a kind of cold rationalization of Christmas and that the fairy tale elements have consciously been given preference. This doesn't happen because of an unchristian intent, but because people become preoccupied with the fabulous and are therefore influenced in an unchristian way in the essentials. I shall illustrate that later with examples. We must be grateful for the fact that the Holy Mother and her child achieve at Christmas time what all the preachers together in the course of a year do not achieve, namely that the world turns for a while with reverent heart toward the crib. But we must nevertheless, for the sake of the gospel, let the purely historical have its say, and, whenever possible, make use of the receptive mood of the Christmas days to tell the world how magnificent the event of Christmas actually is. That is the purpose of this book.

I am not writing a new commentary on the gospels of Matthew and Luke. There are already many good commentaries, and it is not my purpose to increase them by a new one. Rather, I am attempting on the basis of these scholarly commentaries to write what is commonly called a "popularization," and I believe that such a thing is desirable and even necessary. I do not address myself especially to scholars, although I hope scholars will read and judge my work, but rather to everyone who at the feast of Christmas turns toward the crib and asks: How was it really in those times? Are we dealing with fable or reality? And with

1. In Holland, especially in Protestant circles, there is the custom of having religious Christmas gatherings at which the story of Christmas is freely rendered.

which reality? I am thinking of all those who seek God and love the truth. Naturally I don't mean that I will leave scholarship out of consideration altogether—on the contrary, it is my point of departure. I should never have been able to write this book without reference to scholarly material, and I am of the opinion that science and faith are one, indeed must be one, since there is only *one* truth, which it is the duty and task of both faith and science to seek. What is set forth here makes the claim of having adequate scientific grounding. The necessary evidence is abundantly cited. However, I do not rely solely on one commentary. The commentaries often do not agree; in such cases I have made a considered judgment and whenever necessary, have gone my own way.

I come from the evangelical theology and church of the Netherlands, I bring with my approach to the Catholic position the old love for everything that is "biblical," and I confess with gratitude that this old "baggage" is not felt, on the Catholic side, as a strange burden. On the contrary, I find it to be the common element which meets with respect wherever Christians gather. In the attempt to find the truth, different searchers often arrive at different conclusions. Since, however, we are all concerned with truth and nothing else, every contribution from a different mentality is to be considered as gain. For this reason I welcome any comment and viewpoint that others may make concerning the content of my book.

CHAPTER I

THE SO-CALLED CENSUS

Now it came to pass in those days, that there went forth a decree from Cæsar Augustus that a census of the whole world should be taken. This first census took place while Cyrinus was governor of Syria. And all were going, each to his own town, to register.

Luke 2:1–3

IN SEPARATING the real tradition of the Christmas events from its romantic representations, we can begin at that point where the blend of the two becomes clearly and even comically evident, namely in the so-called "census."

There we read: "census," "population census," and "enroll." Why do our translators select the completely inadequate word "census,"[1] which is certainly not called for by the original text, and which biblical scholarship decidedly rejects? The word in the Greek original is *apographe* and means a "writing down," or "registration," not a "counting." Are the translators making a concession to the popular mind which likes to adopt the simplest concept? In this case it would be an unscientific and unhistorical concession, bringing about the very situation mentioned in the Introduction: historical matters are thrust into the background in favor of the unhistorical and the legendary.

1. Translator's note: The passages from the New Testament are taken from the Confraternity edition, 1941. (The author's German NT passages were taken from the 4th edition of the Herder-Bücherei, 1960.)

Let us take a closer look. In the Netherlands, and doubtless elsewhere, a population census is taken every ten years, and the authorities set aside a certain day on which they may assume most everyone will be *at home*, namely on New Year's Eve. Everyone who is not at home at midnight on New Year's Eve makes the census more difficult. It is important for an exact count that as many as possible be at home at this time. Wherever census-taking is practiced, similar principles prevail. Did the Romans in biblical times proceed differently? Probably not. Roman law even in our day is a model of clear, carefully weighed principles which no jurist can ignore. The Roman Empire had a carefully constructed and well organized administrative system which is admired even today. It is unthinkable that a census would have been carried out in the foolish manner suggested by the false translation and interpretation of the biblical text. We cannot in good conscience believe this of the Roman administration, especially in the golden age of Cæsar Augustus.

When as a boy I experienced one of those decennial population counts and was told in school just why this count had to take place precisely at midnight on New Year's Eve, and when in the same week I heard the Christmas stories (naturally, with the word "census"), I wondered why these stories told of an entirely different kind of census by the great emperor. And when I then consulted Schlosser's *World History* and read there of the greatness, the orderliness and exemplary organization of the Roman Empire, the whole thing struck me as odd. For the first time I began to doubt my Christmas narrators, for what they were saying simply couldn't be true. I didn't know then how to solve the problem, but it tormented me for years, especially since doubt in one area breeds doubt in others. I became critical. And this criticism didn't diminish any when I met with surprise, but no answers, from the people I consulted. They apparently didn't know either, and so they blithely continued their prevarications (so it seemed to me at the time) and did so "in the service of the church," as they were wont to say. But neither the church nor my perplexity was served. I continued to say to myself—imagine that kind of a "census" in the biblical lands!

> And all were going, each to his own town, to register. And Joseph also went from Galilee out of the town of Nazareth into Judea to the town of David, which is called Bethlehem—because he was of the house and family of David—to register, together with Mary his espoused wife, who was with child.
>
> Luke 2:3–5

"*All* went," that means here: everyone who was not in "his own city." What does that mean: his own city? For Joseph that meant Bethlehem, for according to tradition King David dwelt in Bethlehem—about a thousand years B.C. . . . Moreover, David also had *his* ancestors. . . . But we'll leave that aside. Are we to conclude then that everyone had to journey to where his "tribal ancestor" lived about a thousand years before? Who was the tribal ancestor of any given Jew who had to be counted; and where had he lived? Or perhaps for other Jews the "tribal ancestor-for-the-census" was, so to speak, not the ancestor from the time of the King David, but rather the ancestor from the time of the alleged division of the land by Joshua? Which ancestor would the Roman governor Cyrenius assign to each Jew? To assign each one his tribal ancestor of a thousand years before would have been quite arbitrary.

But to ascertain the tribal ancestor for the time of Joshua would have been even more difficult; for the boundaries of the Joshua-territory did not coincide with those of the region that Cyrenius governed. Moreover these did not agree with the boundaries of the Davidian territory. And anyway who would know—with the exception of a few families—what tribe he was from, who his ancestor was and where he lived? Cyrenius didn't know, either! We know that in the eighth century B.C., when Samaria was destroyed, a large part of the Jewish people were carried off to Babylonia, and that this happened again in the sixth century B.C., when Jerusalem fell. By that time the traditional tribal distinctions had disappeared. Even in the time of the Kings the tribes of Judah and Benjamin had become one tribe, called Judah. Similarly the ten tribes of the northern kingdom were fused together under the name "Ephraim."

Above all, however, the forced mass migrations of the Jews had serious consequences. The "tribes" for the most part became confused. Lists of names, in so far as any existed, were lost. Some of the Jews who later returned no longer knew to which tribes they originally belonged. Those who had right of membership in a given tribe often could not prove it. For example, in *Esdras* 2:38 we read "the sons of Senaä, 3,630," a number (adding women and children) which comprises no small part of the 50,000 people who returned. Sons of Senaä means "sons of the despised woman," i.e., people without papers, *displaced persons*, people without a homeland, whose membership in Jewry was not at all confirmed. Several "tribes" did not return. Many of the returnees said they belonged to the tribe of Juda because membership in that tribe was advantageous. In brief, the ancient division into tribes was a thing of the past. And if in the days of Cæsar Augustus the ancestry of a given century was an issue, it was for most people a legend of long ago without any meaning for their own lives.

"And all went . . . every one into his own city." If that was supposed to mean: into the city of some tribal ancestor or another, then the task would have remained an unsolved riddle for three quarters of the population. But even so, what could it matter to a Roman where a Jew thought his ancestors lived in any century? And what possible meaning could that have for an alleged "census"? We can hardly assume a special interest on the part of Romans and their governors for the ancestry of ancient Jewish tribes; it is even less believable that in a census in the service of the emperor and the empire they would evince such an interest, especially amid general ignorance of completely altered territorial boundaries.

Furthermore: The land of the Jews was under occupation, the decrees of the occupying power were hated, and every act of sabotage was considered a sacred duty. Just how welcome would an organized census have been that required everyone to go on a journey? The Jews were excellent saboteurs, and they had plenty of opportunity to practice it. They could easily invent ancestors so as to make the journey, or to say they had none, so they could stay at home. And who paid for the journey? The Romans? In that case their ancestral residence would have been a considerable distance away. Did the Jews themselves have to pay? Then each would already be living in his own city. And who was to manage all this? The Romans? The Jews? The confusion would have been inconceivably great. And then to *count* all these people? If under these conditions almost everyone had taken the trip—the town authorities, the police, the bakers, the merchants, the physicians—and if at the same time a great number of foreigners had poured into the cities, what then would have become of civic order? It would have degenerated into chaos, chaos in every respect. As long as the food supplies lasted, a part of the populace would have been delighted over the general disorder, and would have done everything possible to make it greater and more costly.

In Acts 5:37 we read: "After this man [Theudas] rose up Judas of Galilee in the days of the taxing, and drew away much people after him: he also perished, and all, even as many as obeyed him, were dispersed." And this was not just a matter of sabotage.

A great uprising under the leadership of this well-known and active Galilean helped ruin completely the so-called census. We learn from Flavius Josephus that this Judas of Galilee was a versatile and experienced revolutionary. He is said to have formed the party of the zealots, from whose ranks we later meet Simon (Zelotes) among the disciples of Jesus. In *any* year when this so-called census was due we find unrest in the land; this fact alone would have sufficed to make any possible "census" fail completely.

Will perhaps someone object that the Romans didn't know all this? They knew it better than we do now. Or will it be maintained that the Romans knowingly risked all, only to find out how many Jews there were—something they couldn't determine in this fashion anyway? If that really were the case, one need no longer ask why the Roman Empire collapsed. The invasion of the barbarians is usually given as the chief external cause, but the imperial decree in Luke 2:1 would be a much clearer explanation. A realm governed so foolishly would naturally have collapsed within a short period of time. The longer one reflects on it, the more impossible does the interpretation seem which treats all this as a matter of census-taking.

Anyway, there is *nothing* in the history books about a regime, least of all that of the Roman Empire, which had "organized" such a "census."

Don't the Christmas narrators understand all of this? Can't they understand it? To comprehend these things, one need only reflect a bit. Why is it then we still hear again and again of a "census"? Is it because the narrators, just as in telling a fairy story, pleasantly switch off their critical faculty that they may chat romantically and not bother about truth and reality? If that is so—and unfortunately we must admit that the holiday mood finds its expression just this way—then we must oppose this dangerous tendency in the interest of the Good Tidings. For in that case we have not only to deal with an error, but with a false and essentially *unchristian* position.

The error is certainly not in scripture—in the original text we have, as already noted, the word *apographe*, the correct translation of which is "writing down" or "registration" or "taxing" (Acts 5:37), but which—as we saw—needs closer explanation. The *apographe* is not a census; then what is it? The answer is already adequately known. It is clear enough from history and can be found in almost any commentary. It must not be neglected for reasons of comfort or ignored for the sake of a romantic mood. If we wish to formulate the *apographe* in terms of our present-day words and circumstances, then we must make clear that it embraces a double meaning: First, it was what we call today an "assessment of real estate," a listing or registration of the land and dwelling property; for taxation purposes a second meaning is connected with *apographe* (a meaning that *today* is separate from the meaning "assessment of real property") and signifies the assessment of capital worth. This double meaning— assessment of real property and of capital value—cannot today be expressed in *one* word. For people of that day and age the word in the original text was completely clear. For us, who have other administrative systems, an appropriate paraphrase is necessary. This we can arrive at sufficiently clearly on the basis of recovered documents and descriptions.

It is easily understood why the vast empire required a universally valid, official, written registration of property together with a definite official assessment of the monetary value of this property. In those times when there was no industry except for manual trades, the possession of house and land was the criterion for wealth, possessions and income. The tax structure was for the most part erected on this basis. Of course there were other taxes even then, the Romans were never at a loss in inventing taxable objects (e.g., the customs tax, cf. the tax collector, or publican); but the chief tax, in Israel at any rate, was based on this "registration and assessment." The word "registration" is not fully designated by the phrase "taxation of real property"; it was "real property," but it was at the same time "assessment of (individual) capital worth." This double meaning of *apographe* is often combined under the label "census." To understand and explain correctly to others the accounts of Luke and Matthew, it is absolutely essential to have these two meanings before our minds, for only then can the events surrounding the birth of Jesus be sensibly and logically grasped.

The above kind of administration of property had long prevailed in many parts of the Roman Empire during the time of Cæsar Augustus. The statement in Luke 2:1 that the decree went forth that "all the world should be taxed," must not be construed as meaning this practice had never existed before, but rather as meaning that the practice should be continued where it had already prevailed as well as instituted at once where it had not. In the province of the governor Cyrenius or Cyrinus (Latin: Quirinius) it was carried out *for the first time* (cf. Lk 2:2). Up till that time the Jews—more specifically the elders of a city or a village—had regulated their property affairs themselves and, for the most part, by word of mouth. But this practice was unsatisfactory as far as the Romans were concerned, especially since the elders were their enemies and would not reveal the particulars of their real and capital holdings to them. They wished to proceed in a more precise and more "Roman" fashion, an understandable requirement from the Roman point of view. Equally understandable is the uprising under Judas of Galilee (Acts 5:37); since Roman procedures were hated *per se*, and every new decree was a reason for rebellion and resistance, then *this* new decree permitted the Roman authorities to oppress and exploit their Jewish subjects. It is clear why Judas of Galilee drew "much people" after him: his movement was a struggle for freedom, albeit a futile one.

We know from Tacitus (*Annales*, I, 11) and Suetonius (*Octavian*, XX, 101) that such administrative practices had been in force for a long time in the Roman Empire and its colonies. Certain papyri found in Egypt attest to an *apographe* carried out there every fourteen years on the basis of the Roman model (cf. Lk 2:1). The famous inscription in Ancyra (Ankara) mentions three registrations from the years 726, 746, and 767 A.U.C.[2] In Gaul a registration took place in 9 B.C. Judea had its own king, Herod the Great (died 4 B.C.), but he was subject to the Roman government as "rex socius" (=dependent king), and had to conform to Roman law. In 8 B.C. the Jews were even bound by an oath to the emperor, and our biblical "registration" was directed by a *Roman* governor from Syria (the Quirinius mentioned in Lk 2:2). Herod was powerless to stop it.

History tells us that Quirinius became governor of Syria after the exile of Archelaus in the year 6 *after* the birth of Christ. Also, Flavius Josephus says that the taxing of the Jews took place in the year 7 *after* the birth of Christ. Documents (registration formulae) have been found confirming this latter date.

Are we to assume an error on the part of Luke, who is usually a careful historian and who wrote *before* Flavius did (62–63 A.D.)? Or was Flavius in error (he was no friend of Christians) either unintentionally or intentionally?

We need not favor one over the other. Luke and Flavius are both right. For first, it is doubtful whether the translation accurately reproduces the sense of the original. Many think it would be better to translate: "This taxing preceded the taxing which took place under Cyrenius, the governor of Syria." Linguistically this rendition is possible, and if it were conclusive,

---

2. Cf. H. Daniel-Rops, *Jesus and his Times* (New York : Doubleday, 1944). The taxation carried out in the year 746 A.U.C. (*ab urbe condita*, i.e., from the founding of the city [Rome]), is the *apographe* of Luke 2:1. This corresponds with the rest of our dates, as we will see later on.

the Quirinius problem would be fully solved. But it is not con-clusive. Secondly, we possess historical proof of such taxations from the years 6, 20, and 40 of our era. The one in 6 A.D. is fully attested by Flavius Josephus and others. It took place when Archelaus had been deposed: Rome sent a procurator by the name of Coponius to Judea and commissioned Quirinius (Cyrenius) with the taxation proceedings. It is incontestable that Cyrenius was governor of Syria in 6 A.D. Also, this is the taxation referred to in Acts 5:37. It was for Judea the most fateful of all taxations, for the last trace of its so-called independence disappeared after Archelaus' removal from office.

This taxation of 6 A.D. was, however, not the first; the first had taken place fourteen years earlier. It was decreed by the emperor in 746 A.U.C. (=8 B.C.) and is attested both scripturally and by frequent mention of the Jewish resistance against this decree. This resistance lasted many years, and involved continual sabotage and minor unrest that took on the scope of a "rebellion" only after the death of Herod, when the revolutionaries became more daring.

During Herod's time we know of no less than three national heroes who claimed to be the Messias: 1) Judas ben Hiskijahu, or Judas of Galilee, mentioned in the New Testament; 2) Simon of Perea, a former slave of Herod, a handsome man of great physical strength; and 3) a shepherd, likewise of athletic build, with the strange name of Athronges or Athrongaios ("apple of paradise"). The so-called war of Varus put a temporary stop to the whole thing.[3] But even after Jesus there were messianic movements in Israel. Shortly after Jesus' time, Menahem (son of Judas of Galilee) entered Jerusalem leading a well-equipped army

3. See further E. Schürer, *Geschichte des jüdischen Volkes*, 4 vols., 4th ed. 1901–11, Vol. I, pp. 508–543; J. Felten, *Neutestamentliche Zeitgeschichte*, 2 vols., 1910, Vol. I, p. 137–145; Th. Zahn, *Das Evangelium des Lukas*, 1913, p. 129–135, and his *Introduction to the New Testament* (Michigan : Kregel Pub.).

amid loud hosannas, but was assassinated. Later, Andrew the Lycian makes his appearance. And in the reign of the Emperor Hadrian the last uprising, the revolt led by Simon Bar-Cochba ("son of the star"), was of no small significance. It is not surprising that the Emperor Claudius (in a letter to the Alexandrians, discovered in 1929) called Jerusalem the seat of the fever in the national body.

We are concerned in particular with the disturbances associated with the name Judas of Galilee, and their pertinence to the events of Christmas. These disturbances extend from the days of Judas' father, Ezekia, through the life-time of his sons. We may characterize them as a kind of guerilla activity that now and then breaks into open warfare, caused, by the way, not only by the taxations but by many other things: images of the emperor, eagle symbols, an aqueduct passing through sacred temple grounds, the oath of fealty to the emperor, and endless annoying decrees and acts of violence.

Flavius Josephus provides us with more detailed information concerning Judas of Galilee. This Judas, and his father before him, had often caused unrest. When the first taxation was decreed, he made use of this opportunity to start a war of independence. At first he didn't have much success, but after the death of Herod in 4 B.C. he made gains. Flavius writes that he stirred up great unrest and won "a great following" for himself. Supported by Saddok, a Pharisee, he declared that the chosen people no longer need pay taxes to the occupying power, and he aroused furious opposition to the tax registration. He gained control of the city of Sepphoris and was thought by many to be the promised messias. The Roman general Varus departed Syria with two legions, liquidated the followers of Judas in Galilee, turned then to the city of Sepphoris, which he conquered and burned. In so doing he doubtless killed Judas, and sold the surviving inhabitants of Sepphoris into slavery.

This uprising could not prevent the taxation from being carried out nor was it strong enough to be termed a Jewish war of independence; but it had enough force (its suppression required two legions) to cause the Romans considerable difficulty and to delay the taxation for quite a while.

According to Josephus, a certain Judas of Galilee instigated a revolt against the second taxation in the seventh year *after* the birth of Christ. Many are of the opinion that this Judas is the Judas of the Varus war. In itself this is not impossible; he may have escaped alive from Sepphoris. But it is more probable that Judas of Galilee perished in the war with Varus and that the second uprising was staged by Judas' son of the same name.

The question now remains whether Cyrenius was connected with the first tax registration in the years 8 and 7 B.C. At that time Saturninus was the official governor of Syria, but Quirinius in any case was already in Syria at the time; an inscription attests to an earlier Syrian registration by Quirinius in the city of Apamea. Tacitus and Strabo report that Quirinius, as *legatus Cæsaris pro praetore* had to accompany the young Cæsar (an eighteen-year-old grandson of Augustus) during his stay in the East. This was a very special distinction, roughly corresponding to the position of a governor. Tacitus (*Annales*, III, 49) and Strabo (XII, 65) further tell us that at this time (12 to 1 B.C.) Quirinius conquered the warlike tribe of the Homonadensians from the Taurus mountains (in Cilicia). Such a war can only have been conducted by the governor of a nearby province, and Syria alone would come under consideration here. Furthermore, the so-called Tiburtine inscription indicated that "one" (unhappily, the name is not preserved) became governor of Syria a second time; more than likely this refers to Quirinius, as do two inscriptions from Antioch in Pisidia, which attest to Quirinius as ruler in Syria also *before* the birth of Christ.

When Tertullian says that the taxing in Luke 2 took place

under Saturninus, who was the governor of Syria until 6 B.C., we must believe him, for he had access to official documents in Rome. His witness gains in historical value when we realize that the textually faithful Tertullian would only reluctantly have cited a different name from that of Quirinius for the taxing in Luke 2. And yet Tertullian makes no mention of any contradiction in the text of Luke 2:2.

Saturninus was the official governor of Syria when Jesus was born (the birth of Christ was actually in the seventh year *before* our Christian era—we'll have more to say of that later on— and Saturninus was Syrian governor until 6 B.C.). But Quirinius, the former governor, was still (or perhaps, once more) in the near East. The execution of the tax registration, which was "the first" in Judea, took several years. Not the least of reasons for this delay was the sabotage and rebellion under Judas of Galilee. The performance of this really difficult task fell to the lot of Quirinius as *legatus Cæsaris*. As *legatus* he had the same rank as a governor, and was addressed by the latter title because he had already been governor in this region; Luke also uses this title for him.

From the welter of dates the following can now be inferred: In the year 7 A.D. the (second) registration took place (again under Quirinius as governor of Syria), and in keeping with the requirement that every fourteen years an assessment should be held of one's real and capital worth, the beginning of the first registration (Lk 2:1 f.) therefore fell in the year 7 B.C. Since Christ was born 7 years *before* our era, the assertions in Luke's gospel are quite correct.

We can picture the proceedings as follows. A Roman commission, aided by Jewish-Herodian collaborators who knew the country and language, would move through the land and remain a few months in each locale. During the "first" time, the task of making a thorough and reliable check of properties together with the owners and their heirs, was far from easy: every plot of land, every house had to be assessed. Witnesses had to be interrogated, disputes settled, etc. If a village could be "covered" in three months, that was moving pretty fast. To have moved through the entire country in this way must have taken all of fourteen years, and have given the commission reason to allow the two registrations to overlap. Actually it doesn't matter whether Quirinius held the title of Syrian governor in the first or in the second registrations, or even later; in any event it is definite that he was the supervisor of the registration in Luke 2.[4]

> And all were going, each to his own town, to register.
>
> Luke 2:3

The "all" must be taken *cum grano salis*. The followers of Judas of Galilee certainly didn't go, and many who were not actually followers, but sympathetic to his cause, didn't go either. Add to these the ones who were either indifferent as to their possible property rights or regarded them as too slight to be worth the long and expensive journey, plus those people whose interests were handled by proxies in their native cities. But St. Luke is doubtless right in saying the great majority obeyed the decree.

Who did go? Everyone who had possessions in his home town, a share in them, or rights as heirs to such possessions. Hardly anyone would have gone because the Romans demanded it, but only so as not to risk losing his rights and falling prey to the sanctions of Roman law. Also one's absence might permit too high an evaluation to be placed on his goods, and result in heavy taxes to be paid over many years (till the next assessment). To be present at the registration was to help validate one's arguments with the authorities and to keep the evaluation as low as possible.

Of course not everyone took the journey at the same time. The registration commission couldn't be everywhere at the same time.

4. Cf. Th. Zahn, *Das Evangelium des Lukas*, 1913, p. 752 f.

They worked through place by place, city by city and probably "crept" through the land, since the registration of every piece of land took time—especially in Judea, where this was going on for the first time. People knew approximately where the commission was and when it was expected in this or that village or city, where they had to look after their interests. Of course no one knew exactly, and no one was sure whether it was his turn next or whether he would have to wait long to register. Consequently it was wise to be on time and then calmly wait one's turn in his particular locale. Sometimes it was necessary to stay three months, or in the larger cities, even longer.

We can see that these various trips throughout the land must have gone on throughout the fourteen years and that only those people who took the trip expected the commission to be in a certain place and wanted to be present there. Seen from the outside, actually very little would have been noticed of these journeys in the everyday life of the people. Perhaps in the place where at a given time the commission was beginning its work a fairly large crowd of people might have come together, especially in a village like Bethlehem, which had only a small caravansary. But we must not exaggerate even this gathering of people. Bethlehem had at that time approximately 1,200 inhabitants. How many then would there have been who possessed property rights in Bethlehem so as to make such a trip feasible? The number of arrivals cannot have been large, but still too large for the only caravansary in that area.

It is clear how completely amiss the concept "census" would be under these circumstances. To count the people was not the point at all. This expression is least suited for making the events at Christmas understandable and for bringing to life the background in which the Christmas mystery took place. What took place in Bethlehem is now clear. Those people who had property rights there journeyed there to validate these rights for themselves and for their children, and to oversee their evaluation and to assure that their taxes would not be set too high. Only those people were involved who, like Joseph, had to leave their birthplace in order to live and to work somewhere else, but still had rights in their birthplace, whether in the form of possessions, rents from possessions, or inheritances.

> And Joseph also went from Galilee out of the town of Nazareth into Judea to the town of David, which is called Bethlehem—because he was of the house and family of David— to register, together with Mary his espoused wife, who was with child.
>
> Luke 2:4

That Joseph went to Bethlehem means that he had rights there, and that it was to his advantage to leave his workship in Nazareth for a length of time and to represent his case in accordance with the Roman decree. Probably his parents' home was not concerned here at all, for Joseph at this time was about fifty to sixty years old.[5] Doubtless it was a matter of goods as yet undistributed or of rents.

That Luke mentions "the house and lineage of David" does not mean that Joseph's journey had anything to do with the fact that David dwelt in Bethlehem a thousand years before, but rather merely indicates that descendants of David still dwelt in Bethlehem and that also Joseph came from Bethlehem.

Although the carpenter Joseph as a descendant of the royal house of David had no royal riches, it is exaggerated to represent him as particularly poor. He belonged to the middle class. How extensive his rights were in Bethlehem, we don't know, but we must not imagine them as too insignificant. They justified, in any case, a journey of about 93 miles that cost a fair amount of money, as well as an interruption of work in Nazareth that meant a half a year's absence.

5. We shall discuss this more thoroughly later (see Chapter II).

It was a weighty decision for Joseph to start on this journey and to take his young wife with him. The journey took four days. Mary would not have travelled on foot; according to custom Joseph would have provided her with a mule, but the journey would not have been much more comfortable because of that. Furthermore, he had to reckon with the activities of the Judas rebels; the followers of Judas of Galilee probably would not have reached Bethlehem, for near Bethlehem lay a strong fortress of Herod, but even so the trip was not without danger. Also the strain of the trip would be hard on Mary. Joseph had much to consider. But he finally decided in spite of all to go and to take Mary with him.

Joseph doubtless had many reasons for this decision. In the first place he knew that the expected child was a holy one and since he could give this child the rights of the Davidian house, it was not only in his own interest but also in the interest of the child that he represent these rights. This was probably not a regulation, but certainly commendable. It was not necessary for him to "register" Mary, for she had so far as we know no property rights in Bethlehem and probably did not stem—we will come back to this point—from the house of David. But if he did have to register her, then it would have been better for her to have gone to Bethlehem from the house of Elizabeth and, in her condition, spared herself the double journey. Apparently she did not make the proposal to go to Bethlehem. The "registration" concerns Joseph, and him only. But with the expected child the situation was different. This child would be Joseph's heir, and in consideration of this the father acted conscientiously and with the utmost solicitude. He fulfilled his paternal duty with the greatest care.

In the second place, he took the mother of the coming child along with him not only for this reason, but also because he could not leave her alone in Nazareth for such a long period of time. The circumstances of his marriage were not unknown in Nazareth and would gradually have been rumored about. If Mary had remained behind in Nazareth, she would have had to endure a very unpleasant time because of the rumors and gossip in surroundings that were not favorably disposed to her anyway. This journey would afford Mary many a hardship; but to remain alone in Nazareth would have been even harder on her.

That Joseph and Mary were mindful in this connection of the passage in Michah 5:2 (where the birth in Bethlehem is prophesied) is in itself not impossible, but rather improbable. It often happens that the believer understands a prophetic text only after its fulfillment, but the non-believer with his critical or even hostile point of view pays more attention to particulars in the prophecies. Thus the women went on Easter morning with fragrant spices to the tomb in order to anoint the body of the Lord (Mk 16:2; Lk 24:1). However, it occurred to the enemies of Christ that "that deceiver said when he was still alive: 'after three days I will rise again,'" whereupon they asked Pilate for assurance that this resurrection would be prevented. Love is concerned with the immediate things; hostility is distrustful, and, for that very reason, more critical. On the other hand it is not absolutely impossible that Joseph and Mary thought of Bethlehem as the birthplace of the coming Messias according to the promise in Michah 5:2. In any case, they went together and left their home in Nazareth for a considerable time. Possibly Joseph and Mary might even have considered remaining in Bethlehem if the circumstances in Judea had permitted it.

Did both of them know that the journey would involve a lengthy absence from home? Of course. In the first place, they did not leave at a time when the birth of Jesus was imminent. That would have been an impossible demand on both mother and child, one that we cannot impute to either Joseph or Mary. Besides, the Greek word for the days that were "accomplished" (cf. Lk 2:6) refers to a considerable length of time and indicates that the proposed journey was planned on a long range basis. It seems like childish folly whenever the Christmas narrators and Christmas pageants make-believe that the birth took place right after the arrival in Bethlehem. Don't these makers of legends see that they do Joseph, the careful father, a disservice when they make of him a foolish clod who knows no better (at the most significant time for the Holy Maid and for the whole world) than to subject Mary to the rigors of a four day journey, and who even in his native village finally has to go begging for lodgings— right before Mary was to deliver?

Of course, the opposite is true. Joseph departed Nazareth in plenty of time so that Mary would not have to suffer any more than necessary on the journey, and he intended to remain in Bethlehem for a time after the birth. He no doubt left Nazareth not long after Mary's return from her visit to Elizabeth, because he probably wanted to celebrate the Passover in Jerusalem. In Bethlehem he no doubt stayed a few days past the forty-day period after the birth. Consequently we may calculate the stay in Bethlehem as being from four to six months, and more likely four than six. And when he arrived in Bethlehem, the beginning of the tax registration must have been imminent, for the inns were all occupied. He therefore did not arrive any too soon. Then, too, he had to time his arrival just right, for all things considered, the waiting period for *any* participant in the registration could last several months, although of course that could not be known in advance.

Now that we have a clear idea of the registration and its background, we will turn to the most important task of this treatise: to set forth what we know about Joseph and Mary. Even here the romantic imagination has allowed itself free reign; but we can and will liberate ourselves from it.

CHAPTER II

JOSEPH AND MARY

It is not easy to think of the Holy Family in a way that does full justice to the historical facts. The gospels, which of course do not have a scientifically historical purpose, leave much unanswered which was well known and vivid in the minds of the readers at that time from their own experience, but which for us has become a problem after nineteen hundred years. What evidence we encounter is relatively meager; it is therefore all the more important that we consider it carefully.

We meet with special difficulties in the matter of Joseph and his relation to Mary. Often in my life I have had the dubious pleasure of seeing Christmas plays in which the figure of St. Joseph rather resembled a caricature. Now this did not happen because of ill will or even superficial interest; what was portrayed was what people knew or imagined, and that was too little and for the most part decidedly inaccurate. Such a distorted image of Joseph is not necessarily in keeping with the true state of affairs. And as one of the main characters in the most sacred event in the history of the world, Joseph deserves our full attention. We said earlier that Joseph at that time was a man of fifty or sixty years of age. On what can we base this claim?

The last time we hear anything of Joseph in the gospels is when he goes with the twelve-year-old Jesus into the temple. After that he is no longer mentioned. Moreover the gospels do not give the impression that he died particularly young and that Mary became a widow at an unusually early age. On the contrary, we sense from the scriptures that it seemed fitting for Mary to stand beneath the cross alone. If we are right in our assertion that Joseph was already an old man at the time of Jesus' birth, then the evangelists, who knew at first hand what we are now trying to understand, have given a reasonable statement of the circumstances on this point.

We arrive however at a firm historical basis in this matter when we consider more closely the problem of the "brothers and sisters" of Jesus. The texts are familiar. In Mark 6:3 we read "Is not this the carpenter, the son of Mary, the brother of James, and Joseph, and of Jude, and Simon? and are not his sisters here with us?" And Matthew 13:55 f. reads: "Is this not the carpenter's son? Is not his mother called Mary? And his brethren, James, and Joseph, and Simon, and Jude? And his sisters, are they not all with us?" From these two texts in which Jude and Simon are reversed in their order and in which furthermore first a mention is made of sisters and then of "all" sisters (so that at least three sisters must have been meant) we count at least seven brothers and sisters. Moreover, the fraternal name, especially for James the "Just," is often used in the Acts of the Apostles and in the Epistles (Acts 12:17; 15:13; 21:18; 1 Cor 15:7; Gal 1:19; 2:9–12; Jas 1:1; Jude 1:1). And also in the history of the first century this fraternal name appears countless times, e.g. in Flavius Josephus (*Antiquities*, XX, 9, 1), Hegesippus (cf. Eusebius, *Hist. Eccl.* 2, 33) and in many others. A whole library has been written about these brothers and sisters.

The following hypothesis of St. Jerome from the beginning of the fifth century has one considerable support. It states: the "brothers" and "sisters" are male and female cousins or "relatives" of Jesus in the general sense. Jerome based his assertion on the supposition that in Hebrew, and therefore probably in Aramaic, there is no proper word for "male cousin" or "female cousin" and therefore often all relatives were referred to by the designations "brother" or "sister." Here are a few examples: Lot, the nephew of Abraham, is called in Genesis 14:16 his brother; the nephews of King Ahaziah are called in 2 Kings 10:13 his brothers; in Tobias 8:9, Tobias calls his relative Sarah his sister, etc.

We cannot simply dismiss the argument of St. Jerome; we respect his endeavor to put an end once and for all to the legend that Mary had several children after Jesus. But to establish this there are far better arguments. Moreover the argument of Jerome (which, although it is widely held in the Church, is not dogmatic) is subject to a great deal of criticism.

In the first place, the New Testament, as we know now, is for the most part not a translation; the prevalent assumption is today that with the exception of the Matthew gospel it was not written in Aramaic or Hebrew but in Greek.[1] And *this* language has no words for "brother" and "sister" which can be interpreted as also meaning nephew, niece, cousin, or relatives.

Secondly, the Greek translator of the Aramaic Matthew gospel, who knew both languages thoroughly and was also very close to the events in point of time, must have guarded against any possible misunderstanding of the name brother in the case of the other evangelists and of Paul, by means of a careful translation. This would be especially true since he knew that in Jerusalem the brother-concept had taken on dynastic proportions. Under these conditions he doubtless would have used the word for "relative," so as not to mislead his Greek-speaking readers. But he does not do this.

Thirdly, we do not get the impression from reading passages where brothers and sisters are mentioned, that this designation

1. On the question of the language in the original Matthew, cf. the recently published article by J. Kürzinger in *Biblische Zeitschrift*, 1960, pp. 19–38.

is being used in an exaggerated or transferred sense. For example, in Matthew 12: 46 f., "his mother and brothers stood without, desiring to speak with him," we do not feel that these brothers are cousins. Mother and brothers are mentioned here in the same breath. Besides, there were real cousins of Jesus, namely the sons of Salome and Zebedee: James and John (for the scriptural passages, see below). The distinction between "cousins that are called cousins," and "cousins that are called brothers," is not very convincing. Fourthly, the entire history of those early centuries as well as the oldest tradition of the church up to the fifth century contradict the Jeromian hypothesis, and provide a much better explanation.

The problem is very important for two reasons—first, our concern in this book with Bethlehem and the Holy Family. If we wish to obtain a correct picture of Bethlehem and Christmas, then we must examine this problem. Second, the clarification of this matter is important because of the widely held view among Protestant Christians that Mary had several children besides Jesus. Against the Catholic position they base their very confident arguments on Matthew 13:55, Mark 6:3 and elsewhere, and reject the argument of Jerome as weak, manifestly wrong, untenable, and far-fetched;[2] they do this, at times smiling a bit, out of sincere conviction. And so also for this reason it is of crucial significance for us how the relationship of Joseph and Mary is to be interpreted. Without an adequate explanation of this question we would miss one of the most important keys to the understanding of the whole. Consequently, we will probe somewhat more deeply into the problem.

In so doing, we encounter a new difficulty following on the heels of the Jeromian one. Apparently with the intent of supporting Jerome's argument, the attempt was made to interpret the

2. Exceptions are, e.g., V. Taylor, *The Historical Evidence for the Virgin Birth*, 1921, and J. Gresham-Machen, *The Virgin Birth*, 1930.

brothers of Matthew 13:55 and Mark 6:3 as actual cousins. This comes about as follows. In John 19:25 we have: "Now there stood by the cross of Jesus his mother, and his mother's sister, Mary [the wife] of Cleophas, and Mary Magdalene." The question is: How many women are mentioned here, three or four? The proponents of the Jeromian hypothesis say: three. They consider "his mother's sister, Mary the wife of Cleophas" to be *one* person, so that Mary's sister is likewise named Mary. However, that the two sisters both would have had the name Mary is improbable even in Israel, if not impossible.

The interpretation cannot be vindicated by referring to a dynasty name such as Herod (or Napoleon); these are real dynasty names. The name Mary is not that; moreover the names of the various "Herods" were designated by special surnames, such as Herod Antipas, Herod Philippus, Herod Agrippa, and Herod without a second name. They further assume that this Mary of Cleophas (this can also mean, by the way, the mother or daughter of Cleophas) is the *wife* of Cleophas, and they identify this Cleophas with Alphaeus, and identify James, the "brother of the Lord," with James Alphaeus, and in this manner conclude that Jesus and his brothers and sisters are really cousins; of the *five* persons that in the New Testament bear the name of James, there are thus only *two* left!

It is not our purpose or task here to delve deeply into this interpretation, but in order to form an opinion, three of the more important points on this question should be brought out, namely:

First, we have already noted that in Israel it was even more unlikely than it is with us that two sisters would be called Mary. Not three, but *four* women stood near the cross of Jesus:

1) Mary, the mother of Jesus; 2) the sister of his mother, whom John in his well-known diffidence does not mention by name, but only in this indirect way; she is known to us from Mark 15:40; 16:1 as Salome, the wife of Zebedee and mother of the

disciples James and John; 3) Mary of Cleophas; and 4) Mary of Magdola or Mary Magdalene.

Second, even if the Mary of Cleophas is the latter's wife (a fairly reasonable assumption), Cleophas is not identical with Alphaeus. The Aramaic or Syro-Chaldaic translation of the Greek name Klopa, Klopas or Kleophas is Klepoja, and Alphaeus is rendered in those languages as Chalphai.

Third, in the New Testament there are not two, but *five* persons with the name James, which might be reduced to four, but not to two. We find 1) James, the brother of John, son of Zebedee and Salome, the cousin of Jesus; 2) James, the son of Alphaeus (Mt 10:3; Mk 3:18; Lk 6:15 and Acts 1:13), who after St. Jerome was wrongly identified with James the brother; 3) James, also the son of a Mary (Mt 27:56; Mk 15:40 and Lk 24:10), who had the surname "the Little" (*Mikros*, meaning "small," and apparently referring to his small stature; it does not mean "minor"—the Less—as has been erroneously construed); 4) a James who was the father of one of the Twelve (Mt 10:3; Mk 3:18; Lk 6:16; cf. Jn 14:22); and finally 5) James, the brother of the Lord. We meet him in Matthew 13:55; Mark 6:3; Acts 12:17; 15:13; 21:18; 1 Corinthians 15:7; Galatians 1:19; 2; 9:12; James 1:1; Jude 1:1. It is really a complicated job of exegesis to sort out completely these five Jameses on the basis of the cited texts *and* the oldest tradition. Anyway, whether or not out of these five men named James we make four is immaterial for our present purpose, as long as the last-mentioned James, the brother of the Lord, is in no case identifiable with any one of the others.

Special care must be taken not to identify James, son of Alphaeus with James, the Lord's brother. We are of the opinion, for very cogent reasons of which some have already been noted, that James of Alphaeus is an entirely different person from James, the Lord's brother, and with a completely different history.

Besides the reasons noted above, we may point out that the son of Alphaeus was among the Twelve when the Lord's brother still denied Jesus; the latter James was not converted until *after* the resurrection (1 Cor 15:7). Alphaeus' son had outside of Palestine an entirely different history than did James the brother, who lived and died in Jerusalem. Also, the son of Alphaeus is not a cousin of Jesus.

The untenable interpretation that we have criticized above certainly ought not to be advanced in opposition to all the evidence merely to make Jerome's weak arguments to some degree more acceptable by means of a "cousin hypothesis." Such an interpretation is very cramped, and actually weakens the Jeromian hypothesis more than it strengthens it—indeed, it is rather a proof *against* that hypothesis. Nor is it necessary to "rescue" Jerome's interpretation. Jerome is holy, but not his hypothesis; anyway, it is of minor worth in comparison with the other great achievements of this famous saint. If the Church has held to this hypothesis almost exclusively, she is surely not bound by it, and above all she has never given it any dogmatic consequence whatsoever.

According to this earliest Church tradition, which enjoyed universal acceptance during the first four hundred years, the brothers and sisters of Jesus are really just that, except that they are step-brothers and step-sisters. And the ancient reports are certainly not mistaken when they (in Greek!) speak of the *adelphos*, the brother (James the Just) always with a special reverence. It is even striking how in the community at Jerusalem a kind of "Jesus-dynasty" was maintained in which Davidian ancestry played no small role. As the Latin historians tell us, this "dynasty-nimbus" was so strong that the Emperor Domitian (81–96) ordered the leaders at that time of this "dynasty" (two grandsons of the brother Jude, elders of the Church in Pella-Jerusalem) brought to Rome that he might determine whether a new "king" of the Jews was to be feared, and therefore perhaps another Jewish war. When the emperor had seen and listened to these two men and noticed their rough, workmen's hands, he was satisfied and sent them home.

Noteworthy, too, is the fact that the epistles of James and Jude, the two brothers, have become canonical. This entire aura of dynasty is related to the actual, justifiable use of the name of brother, and would be totally inexplicable by Jerome's hypothesis.

But these brothers and sisters of Jesus are by no means children of Mary. They were too old to be. When James (according to Flavius Josephus) in 62 A.D. was hurled down from the walls of the temple, he was ninety-six years old. There are no grounds for doubting this assertion—on the contrary, it is confirmed elsewhere. In the year of Jesus' birth—even considering the fact that our Christian time reckoning is too late by seven years (see below)—James was therefore twenty-seven years old, and hence considerably older than his alleged mother Mary. His brother Simon or Simeon was about James's age. And the fact that two grandsons of the brother Jude were in Rome in the eighth decade A.D. correspondingly speaks for an advanced age for Jude. Jesus' brothers and sisters were therefore all quite a bit older than Mary, who according to all indications must have been about eighteen years old at the time of her marriage to Joseph.

And so we acknowledge the early Church tradition, which was in general acceptance before Jerome's time and which for the foregoing reasons suggests itself so strongly to us, that it can only seem strange that the theological world has not long ago recognized its worth.

Furthermore, it would be possible on the basis of this tradition to clarify and simplify the problem of Mariology in the dialogue with those of the Protestant faith. It is surprising that the latter have so seldom examined this question in the light of the

statements by Flavius Josephus. For the most part they leave
matters as they were, explain that Jesus' brothers and sisters were
born of Mary, and do not bother to examine the consequences
of James the Just having met his death in his nineties (62 A.D.).
The early Church was much more aware of all this than we are.
That on the one hand she hands on to us an image of Mary that
agrees in all points with the later Mariology, but on the other
hand casually mentions brothers and sisters of Jesus, confirms
once more that we have understood history correctly on this
point, and that—this is of paramount importance for our
analysis—in this way we can arrive at a true picture of the
relationship of Joseph and Mary.

Since Joseph's eldest son was twenty-seven to twenty-eight
years old at the time of his father's marriage to Mary, then
Joseph must have been *at that time fifty to fifty-five years of age
or older.*

This agrees with the impression we get from the gospels. It is
also—to mention something now that is often overlooked, but
of great importance to us—in accord with the idea we get of
the character of, first, the brothers of Jesus (especially the eldest,
James the Just) and then of their father Joseph—both in scripture
and history. That is to say, of Joseph we know, unfortunately,
relatively little; of the brothers we know more, especially of
James. Just as we can know the son through his father, can we
not also learn of the father from his sons? It would be helpful to
investigate more closely these two men, James and his father
Joseph, as well as the question of why and in what sense Joseph
is called in the gospel "just," or "righteous" (cf. Mt 1:19). The
father of Jesus deserves this appellation, and so does James, the
great and venerable leader of Christianity in Palestine. We must
limit ourselves to brief references, but it will become evident
how much we can gain in an understanding of Joseph and his
relation to Mary.

James, who enters history as "the Just," commanded considerable influence in the region of Palestine, an influence extending as far as Egypt and Arabia, and which gained for him in Jerusalem (although this is not to be attributed to any possible compromises there) a respected place even in the eyes of the Jewish authorities. This respect remained undiminished until the year 62 A.D. when he refused to take part in the war preparations of the Jews against the Romans. He met his death then at the hands of the war fanatics. He was an extraordinary person.

The Acts of the Apostles recites chiefly the doings of Peter and Paul and makes almost no mention of the other apostles or of James, but this does not mean that James, the brother of the Lord, did not occupy a position equal in importance to that of Peter and Paul. James was the leader of a very far reaching mission in Palestine, Asia Minor, and Egypt, and achieved in the east as much as Paul did in the west. We know quite a bit about James, chiefly from Flavius Josephus. His whole life is a rich commentary on the little we know of Joseph, and enables us to gain an initial understanding of the Holy Family.

James and Joseph are both characterized by their reverence for the Old Testament and the old traditions. Only in the light of this attitude is it clear why James, the leader of the Church in Jerusalem, was allowed to carry on his work unmolested, while Stephen was stoned to death, the Christian community, with the exception of the apostles (Acts 8:1), was scattered, and Paul nearly killed by hostile Jews in Jerusalem and liberated only with difficulty by Roman soldiers. This is not to say that James remained unmolested because of cowardice or concessions to his enemies; he was a man of firm character and unshakeable conviction. But he was a "Jewish Christian," and his reverence for the temple and the law so genuine and honest that he commanded the respect of even the most fanatic Jew. They respected him if only because he was James, son of Joseph of the house of David.

Joseph lived according to the same principles. We will have opportunity later to attest this in detail. Thus, Joseph, after the visit of the magi, stayed in Bethlehem until the forty days elapsed when he could go into the temple with Mary and her son. Both James and Joseph are distinguished by their great calm, maturity of judgment, foresight and determination. It is by no means accidental that history uses the word *dikaios*, i.e. "just," or "upright," to characterize both men.

The fact that they have so strikingly much in common in character and attitude only strengthens our trust in the oldest tradition of the Church. Both display the same nobility of character, the finest nobility that one can ascribe to the house of David in those times. Both father and son know the proper time to be silent and exercise restraint, but also know when to act quickly and decisively as they see their obligation. The son delayed a long time before he became a follower of Jesus. He did not stand at the cross, but Jesus appeared expressly to him after the resurrection (1 Cor 15:7), a sign of his love for this long absent "brother." Then James acknowledged Jesus and became one of the greatest among the Apostles. Joseph, his father, is like him: slow and deliberate in reaching decisions, but courageous and never wavering nor hesitant when the time comes to act.

It has been objected that it is odd that Jesus entrusted John, not James, with the care of his mother and desired that she stay with John. But that need no longer be surprising. For in the first place we know at that time Jesus' brothers and sisters were not close to him, and second, Mary was not a blood relative of James, whereas Salome and her sons were. Third, Salome's sons were personally very close to Jesus. Moreover, John had a spacious dwelling in Jerusalem.[3] James and the other brothers

---

3. John 19:26 mentions that John took Mary up *eis ta idia*, i.e., into his own dwelling; if Galilean fishermen had their own house in Jerusalem, that indicates a certain degree of comfortable living.

and sisters lived in Galilee, and did not come to Jerusalem until later.

At his betrothal to Mary, Joseph was a man of at least fifty to fifty-five years of age, and had already lived in Nazareth a long time. His children by the first marriage are all mentioned in the gospels as living in or near Nazareth. He knew Mary from her childhood. When, after all his children had left their parental home, Joseph asked Mary to make her residence with him, he had surely given the matter much thought; his views and Mary's must have seemed to him in full accord, and such an accord was reached on a "righteous" basis. It should be noted that all this precedes the announcement of the angel, and therefore must not be understood in the light of later events. We must try to understand Joseph and Mary in terms of what we have noted above. This approach has been surprisingly neglected, and yet is one that yields rich results. The key, however, to the full understanding of Mary—and of Joseph as well—is the Annunciation.

Now in the sixth month the angel Gabriel was sent from God to a town of Galilee called Nazareth, to a virgin betrothed to a man named Joseph, of the house of David, and the virgin's name was Mary. And when the angel had come to her, he said, "Hail, full of grace, the Lord is with thee. Blessed art thou among women." When she had seen him she was troubled at his word, and kept pondering what manner of greeting this might be. And the angel said to her, "Do not be afraid, Mary, for thou hast found grace with God. And behold, thou shalt conceive in thy womb and shalt bring forth a son; and thou shalt call his name Jesus. He shall be great, and shall be called the Son of the Most High; and the Lord God will give him the throne of David his father, and he shall be king over the house of Jacob forever; and of his kingdom there shall be no end." But Mary said to the angel, "How shall this happen, since I do not know man?" And the angel answered and said to her, "The Holy Spirit shall come upon thee and the power of the Most High shall overshadow thee; and therefore the Holy One to be born shall be called the

Son of God. And behold, Elizabeth thy kinswoman also has conceived a son in her old age, and she who was called barren is now in her sixth month; for nothing shall be impossible with God." But Mary said, "Behold the handmaid of the Lord; be it done to me according to thy word." And the angel departed from her.

Luke 1:26–38

Mary, who had previously bound herself with a vow, and who had arranged her life accordingly—this very maid would bear a child, conceived by the Holy Spirit! She who had placed virginity above motherhood, and thereby (we must understand this) was deprived of the friendship of her surroundings, would now receive in her life motherhood in its most sacred meaning. What she heard in those few moments was, to say the least, deeply disturbing, and completely different from what she had hitherto contemplated. Yet here lay the answer to her readiness for a life of devotion. Her life was to have been consecrated to God but she had not known just how. She now heard, and her youthful ideal had attained its highest imaginable fulfillment: Hail, full of grace, you have found favor of God. What she had discussed with Joseph and agreed upon was still good; the angel spoke of the throne of David and with this gave approval to Joseph's custody and name; but Mary's readiness was now being summoned in a way that she had not expected. We can well understand her astonished question: "How shall this be . . . ?" But then her words—"seeing I know not man"—are quite remarkable, and for purposes of our discussion must be examined as to their proper interpretation.

The English word "know" may perhaps be variously interpreted, but the Greek unmistakably means: "since I will have no sexual intercourse with a man." If she had intended merely to say to the angel that she had had no sexual intercourse during her betrothal, her question "How shall this be?" would have been foolish. For Mary knew that in two or three months she would be legally married. Psychologically, therefore, this interpretation is impossible. The angel was saying what would happen in the future. Mary understood this quite well. She was by no means a "stupid child," who would reply to such an important announcement by ignoring the facts. Her question "How shall this be?" was quite literal and precluded any notion of sexual union in the future.

It should also be noted, as commentaries of all persuasions assure us, that in Israel marital rights normally began with the betrothal, so that in Mary's case—assuming a normal state of affairs—sexual relations may be assumed already to have taken place. When Mary therefore says that she "knew no man," she could have reference to an already valid marital state, in the physical aspect of which she would be denying having participated. She does not say this to inform the angel of something he couldn't know—the content of the dialogue reveals the contrary. The angel knows, and Mary speaks with him in the full awareness that he knows all that is in her mind. Nor does Mary mean a temporary situation, for it would then be pointless to ask: "How *will* this happen, since I do not now . . ."

The question makes sense only on the assumption that, in keeping with Mary's convictions, it is impossible that she conceive a child in the foreseeable future, and that both the angel and Mary herself know the *reason* for this impossibility. The reason is—and hence Mary's question to the angel—that she has not had, nor ever will have sexual intercourse in her marriage and therefore cannot expect a child.[4] It follows from this that Mary and Joseph must have discussed this matter previously and were in full accord on it. We therefore agree with the conventional

4. So (among others) M. J. Lagrange, *Evangile selon Saint Luc*, 4th ed. 1927, p. 32 f.

interpretation (usually set forth by Catholic exegetes) of Mary's words: that she would keep to her vow of virginity.

K. H. Schelkle writes: "For some time now Catholic exegetes have also attempted another explanation (thus Paul Gaechter, Romano Guardini, Josef Schmid, Josef Weiger, and others) . . . The old Latin translation renders Luke 1:34: *quoniam non virum* cognovi (*have* known), which reading also Ambrose and Jerome suggest. Tatian also appears to have so construed it[5]." In fact there is another interpretation possible if Mary replies with a past tense verb (*cognovi*) to the future verb used by the angel. But this is neither the usual nor the best authenticated interpretation, and it does not fit as well into the sense of the whole. To the future used by the angel Mary reacts with words that have future *content*. For this reason the newer attempts at explanation are not convincing, in my opinion. Besides, considering the entire context they seem quite unnecessary, and throw no new light on the events. But we now come to the most important point.

If our exegesis of Mary's words is correct, and she and Joseph had entered upon an agreement, what is the significance of this agreement?

The decision of Joseph and Mary would be, says K. H. Schelkle, "one quite extraordinary in Israel . . . Rather, would not marriage seem to her [Mary], as to all Israel, a divinely instituted relationship, and parenthood as willed by God (as in Gn 1:28)? For Mary would then share in the promise of Israel, whose tribes, if they could not witness the salvation of the Messias in their own generation, nevertheless hoped to experience it vicariously in tribes to come of their children and children's children." That was Israel's trust. If a young woman refused of her own volition to share in this trust, this would be denounced by the pious as unbelief.

And further on: If Mary had different views from those of the

5. K. H. Schelkle, *Die Mutter des Erlösers. Ihre biblische Gestalt*, 1959, p. 50 f.

Israelitic belief, "why then did she become betrothed and contract a marriage? According to the Jewish matrimonial laws of the Talmud and the Mishnah, a proposal of virginity in marriage would be unthinkable and without effect. At the most a man might be permitted to postpone the marital state for a time, perhaps for the purpose of studying the Torah. The woman, however, had no such right. She was the handmaid of the man."[6]

Imagine in the light of the foregoing how it would be if such a resolve had been agreed upon by two *young* people! One might say that Mary, if she had taken a vow to deny herself marriage and children (in the eyes of her compatriots a very questionable vow), would have really made an ideal nun. Well and good, but the young man? He would have been an ideal monk, who for his part would find in strict asceticism his highest ideal. Were we to transfer this view of a much later age back to Joseph and Mary (historically considered, a dubious transfer), we then meet the difficult question: Why would a "nun" and a "monk" prior to the Annunciation (which they could not foresee) want to enter into marriage? To risk temptation with such close proximity? That would be neither Christian, nor "righteous" by Old Testament standards. Such an intention is not in keeping with either the character of the honorable Joseph or of Mary.

We take the view that the word of Mary to the angel presupposes a rule of sexual abstinence on the part of both Joseph and Mary. This view, however, is not compatible with the notion that Joseph at that time was still a young man.

But from all of our preceding analysis we are convinced that Joseph was well advanced in years, had by a first marriage at least seven children who had grown up and gone, and that as an elderly and lonely widower he therefore asked Mary, whose person and convictions he knew, to share his dwelling with him

6. Schelkle, p. 49 f.

and to become his wife. For all this there is a perfectly healthy and natural explanation, and we have new and important reasons to be glad that the Jerome-hypothesis is not an obstacle, since all of the possibilities for this explanation are offered in the oldest tradition of the Church.

It is not unnatural at an advanced age to intend having no more children. One can thoroughly understand this in the case of a strong willed, mature, and wise man like Joseph, and one can trust him in his resolve.

It is harder for us to see what prompted Mary in her resolve, although of course Joseph knew at the betrothal. The angel calls her "full of grace" (Lk 1:28). Certainly such a title cannot have been uttered by a divine messenger without reason. Also it is safe to assume that Mary's intent cannot have been, as we mentioned before, thought of in Nazareth as being "full of grace" —on the contrary. In Israel, to value a young woman's virginity more highly than her motherhood was unthinkable.

"Certainly celibacy is understandable in such unusual figures as Elias and Elisha. Also chaste widowhood was esteemed, as in the case of Judith (Jud 16:22) or the prophetess Anna (Lk 2:36 f.). If in New Testament times voluntary celibacy was practiced, it was mostly outside of the Jewish religious community and apparently for reasons running counter to Israel's beliefs."[7] When Mary's relative Elizabeth was childless, she called that a "reproach among men" (Lk 1:25). Mary's position can rest only on religious grounds, but she doubtless found little understanding of it in her community; quite the opposite, it must have scandalized many. She was the "maverick," who offended popular opinion. The angel salutes her as "full of grace," and thereby confirms her faith and life of faith, but such recognition she will *not* have encountered in Nazareth.

7. Schelkle, p. 49.

On the other hand it is hard to imagine the elderly Joseph taking a young girl into his home solely for the possible help she would be in working around the house. It would have been far more fitting for the elderly man to seek out an older woman for this purpose. His reasons must have been of another and deeper sort.

This impression grows on us when we consider Mary's place in the community of Nazareth. If as a betrothed woman her declaration to the angel, ". . . since I know not man," would offend popular sentiment in general, it follows that her attitude would meet with opposition in her village. How could it be otherwise? She was different from the others. Mary doubtless stood alone, and when Joseph later took her with him to Bethlehem, he must have known quite well how difficult things would have been for the defenseless young woman in Nazareth. Mary was independent. The independence with which she undertakes the journey to Elizabeth seems to confirm this. But presumably she was considered strange in her village. This must have been so if her resolve, which ran counter to tradition, was known there, as it no doubt was.

So we may assume that this independence and unique behavior must have caused quite a stir among the villagers, who would not lightly accept this sort of thing from a young person. Mary's place in the community could be likened to that of many young girls in the Middle Ages who were burned as witches, only for having incurred popular resentment. Who knows what Mary may have experienced in her village because of her religious opinions! This is conjectural, but not unfounded. And when we try to understand what moved Joseph to take this young girl to him, her very plight seems the most likely explanation. We do not imagine the righteous Joseph as one who would use the outcast situation of the young girl to his own advantage; selfish motives would contradict all that we know of him. We do not know if Mary's parents were still living then, but probably she was quite alone, and her sister Salome was already married.

It seems to us that Joseph was concerned about this girl when Mary's plight had worsened to the point where a strong hand was necessary. Naturally his concern would grow out of respect for Mary's religious convictions, so completely rejected by others. *He will protect the girl and her vow of virginity.* This is the best way to picture Joseph. He is quite worthy in the eyes of her who is full of grace, and this finds expression in the betrothal. Mary does not refuse his protection. Who knows how greatly in need of Joseph's help she may have been! She fully accepts the protection of this highly respected man of David, of the righteous, elderly Joseph; she knows that she can and may do this without fear. On her part she can also aid and serve this honored man in his loneliness.

Thus we gain a clear picture, a picture which affords a good and historically accountable basis in Mariology, for all further considerations. In brief, it is a special grace of God that Joseph at that time was rather old and could thus set different goals for his betrothal and marriage than could a younger man. He could now as a Davidite secure for the promised Child a royal lineage, legally and as a foster father during his growing years.

The question of whether Mary after the birth of Jesus had sexual relations with Joseph—we are thinking here of the customary Protestant interpretation—is a quite superfluous one. If the angel terms Mary's virginity, vowed as a young girl, as "full of grace," then she can only regard herself as strengthened in her position. Besides, the Protestant interpretation is quite incorrect because the alleged children of Mary were so much older than she was that she could not be their mother. These two great persons in God's plan of salvation live on quite a different plane. They do not come together out of either universally human or even purely accidental reasons. We would do them an injustice to assume that! And the way which we have taken up till now in our essay leads clearly and unambiguously to these rich conclusions. We are grateful for them: The events of Christmas take on a profound meaning.

And Mary hears even greater things. She who is familiar with the history and the promise of her nation hears that the power of the Highest will overshadow her and that the holy thing born of her will be called the Son of God. Says Schelkle, " 'Overshadow' is a mysterious and veiled expression for the work of God. It is an infrequent word and is not used here by chance. We read it in the Old Testament (Ex 40:35, and elsewhere) referring to the cloud over the tabernacle of the covenant, which signified God's mighty presence. 'The cloud overshadowed the tabernacle, and the tabernacle was filled with the glory of the Lord.' Such an overshadowing happened now to Mary through the power of God, and brought about the conception of life."[8] All the more do we marvel at Mary's resolute answer: she does not laugh skeptically as did Sara, Abraham's wife; she asks no new questions, although her heart conceals so many; she answers with complete devotion: "Behold the handmaid of the Lord; be it unto me according to thy word."

And Joseph? We shall learn that Mary did not tell him of the annunciation, and why she did not. He, too, sees himself confronted with an entirely different situation from what he had anticipated; she whom he had thought to be a virgin consecrated to God, now confronts him as a mother.

Inasmuch as the announcement of the wonderful birth of John, the precursor of Jesus, had already broken into the natural stream of history, it is clear that the angel did not have anything less significant to tell Mary; the wondrous news imparted to Elizabeth maintains its meaning only in connection with the even more wondrous thing that would happen to Mary. Why, in the final

8. Schelkle, p. 40.

analysis, should anyone contest the miraculous birth of Jesus?
Whoever tries to grasp the miraculous manifestation of
Jesus Christ on the purely natural level will retain very little of
value either of that or of the *entire* New Testament. Whoever
believes in the miracles of Jesus, in his "wonder"-ful person, his
"wonder"-ful words, and his appearances after his resurrection
will find it "natural" that even the beginning of the life of the
"Word become flesh" must be supernatural. For us, too, a
Magnificat is fitting, and whoever does not grasp this well is
far removed from the heart of Christianity.

Mary was, so far as we know from history, not from the line
of David. The gospels say clearly in several places that Joseph
belonged to the house of David. They tell us nothing of a like
ancestry of Mary, but would certainly have done so—motives for
it would have been numerous—if besides Joseph she too were a
descendant of this house. Allusions concerning her ancestry point
to priestly forebears, and so to the tribe of Levi. Her relative
Elizabeth belonged to the "daughters of Aaron" (Lk 1:5), and
Mary is explicitly designated as her relative (Lk 1:36), for which
Luke uses the word *syngenis*; the word means: belonging to the
same blood. Accordingly, Mary is of priestly descent. According
to Zahn[9] the oldest tradition speaks of her father as the "priest"
Joachim—and of her mother Anna. Ischodad, a well-known
Nestorian bishop of ca. 850 A.D.,[10] says in his famous commentaries that Elizabeth was the sister of Mary's mother, therefore
her aunt; that may be so. In any case Mary and Elizabeth seem to
know each other quite well.

Even in the old days—Justin the Martyr was the first—attempts
were made to include Mary in the house of David, and many still
hold this view today, which however cannot displace the older

9. Th. Zahn, *Kommentar zum Neuen Testament*, Vol. III, p. 76.

10. See Ischodad, the English edition of his commentaries (on Luke 1 and 2).

interpretation.[11] Certainly it is incorrect to cite Paul here as a witness. Paul says in Romans 1:3: "Jesus, which was made of the seed of David according to the flesh." Even Justin appeals to this text. But it must be realized that Paul uses the word "flesh" in a variety of meanings. With him even the "law" is "flesh," as opposed to the spirit. In Paul's use the word "flesh" in Romans 1:3 in no way means what Justin, and after him many others, thinks it means. For Paul the legal descent of Jesus from David's house through Joseph is an "according-to-the-flesh-from-David's-house-forthcoming." Thus Paul intends it, and he cannot be cited as evidence for Justin's view without straining his words.

The endeavor to associate Mary with the house of David seems in the history of the Church to have been motivated more by feeling than by the facts. But whether feeling in this case is right is very questionable. In general it can be said that such a feeling is too little concerned as to what meaning for the Old and New Testaments the words "law" and "right" have. According to law and right Jesus is son of David, and that is of no less consequence than "according to flesh and blood." Whoever does not recognize this, misunderstands the Bible. Law and right are values which perhaps lie outside of the express realm of feeling, but a feeling which does not take these values into account moves in a false direction and deteriorates easily into sentimentality.

The desire, based on a theologically as well as historically imprecise viewpoint, to "raise" Mary to a Davidite, also seriously restricts Joseph's significance. In the gospels, for example in the genealogies in Matthew and Luke with their clear and un-ambiguous formulation "Jesus, the son of Joseph," it is emphatically stated that the Davidian ancestry of Jesus came about legally through Joseph.

Nor should we forget that all this finds its full confirmation in

11. Cf. Lagrange, *Evangile selon Saint Luc*, 1927, p. 37, where he argues the Davidian ancestry of Mary.

the circumstances of the times in which Matthew and Luke were writing. If the Davidian ancestry of Jesus through Joseph had been in dispute, then the gospels would have been of little value in the struggle with the Jews of Palestine. The opposite is the case: they never contested this point, and the relations with the Jerusalem dynasty, which we have already pointed out, emphasize that this ancestry was general knowledge. It is true that in Luke's gospel Mary occupies a more central place of interest while Joseph remains in the background, whereas in Matthew more of a "Joseph tradition" is stressed. Nevertheless, the gospels do not differ in their formulation of the genealogy ("Jesus, the son of Joseph"), and so the assumption gains strength that the Davidian ancestry of Jesus rests on his being Joseph's son.

A parenthetical observation concerning the accounts of Matthew and Luke is not out of place here. Luke was not a Jew. According to Eusebius and Jerome he came from Antioch in Syria, was a pagan by birth and a physician by calling. In Colossians 4:10 f. Paul enumerates his Jewish companions; in verses 12–14 he mentions Luke among those who are of heathen origin. Luke belongs to the first *Gentile* Christians from Antioch. Luke 1 and 2, however, bear a strongly Semitic stamp. Luke's account of Christ's childhood is, according to Schelkle, "Hebraic in style and content. The simple Aramaic style is still clearly recognizable beneath Luke's Greek translation. . . . The three songs of Zacharias, Mary, and Simeon . . . are formed from the spirit and themes of the Old Testament. The Hellenist Luke . . . is not the creator of these narratives. The Palestinian-Judaic local color, the spirit and religiosity of Jewry, could not be depicted by a Luke, who comes from the Gentile Christianity of Antioch. The gospel of Luke announces the coming kingship of God in 1:32–33 as: 'and the Lord God shall give unto him the throne of his father David: and he shall reign over the house of Jacob for ever.' In the rest of Luke's gospel the kingship of God is free from such national-Judaic limitation. The gathering and shaping of the accounts in Luke 1 and 2 must therefore go back to a man who as a pious Jew was at one time associated with the temple and the law. . . . A Jew, not a Greek, is the original narrator."[12]

Josef Schmid says in his commentary on Luke 1 and 2: "Luke cannot himself be the creator of these accounts, for the Palestinian-Judaic local color and the religious viewpoint of the participants is set forth with a degree of authenticity unattainable by a Hellenist. These passages betray such an exact knowledge of everyday life among Palestine Jews, their mores, customs, and manner of thought, that only a Palestinian can have created them. Besides the notion that God, true to his covenant, is now ushering in the age of the Messias, there is also peculiar to these accounts a great emphasis on the religious elements of Judaism, of the temple and law, i.e., things which had already lost their significance for the non-Jewish Christian readers of Luke."[13]

We are fully in accord with this. Luke 1 and 2 have a Jewish source, but this "source" is not a man, but rather a woman, namely Mary. Luke says that he decided "to write . . . in order . . . all things from the very first" (Lk 1:3). And he did that in Jerusalem, where Mary lived; naturally, he spoke with her. It is to Mary, of course, that we owe the account of the conversation between the angel and her; no one else could have told about it. Luke 1 and 2 reveal to us the heart and soul of the holy maid. Of course, Luke had other word-of-mouth sources besides Mary. He even found many eye-witnesses, for most of the persons named in the gospels were still alive. Of the five hundred witnesses that Paul mentions in 1 Corinthians 15:6, the great majority according to him were still alive at the time he

12. Schelkle, p. 58 f.

13. J. Schmid, *Das Evangelium nach Lukas*, 2nd ed. 1951, p. 71.

wrote the letter to the Corinthians, and could therefore be approached for information.

Luke may have gotten particulars from Joanna, the wife of Herod's steward (Lk 8:3), and Manaen, who had been brought up with Herod (Acts 13:1). He met nearly all of the Apostles, first in Antioch, then in Jerusalem and later also in Rome. He also had written testimony at his disposal. The gospel of Mark had already been written; he knew it and made use of it. The original Aramaic version of the Matthew gospel was likewise available, but it is uncertain whether he knew this language. Yet he misses no opportunity in telling of the women who played a role in the events of salvation; in this particular Luke's gospel becomes a "gospel of women."

Luke lets us know quite a bit about Mary. He also "draws" us a picture of Elizabeth, the prophetess Anna, the widow from Naim, the sinful woman, Martha and Mary, as well as of Dorcas, Sapphira, Priscilla, Drusilla, Bernice, Lydia, Damaris, and others (in the Acts of the Apostles), and he knows how to sketch them so well that he became the patron of Christian painting. The painters of the Middle Ages and the Renaissance borrow their favorite themes from his gospel: the annunciation, the visit to Elizabeth, the adoration of the shepherds, the presentation in the temple, the twelve-year-old Jesus in the temple, the woman taken in sin, the disciples at Emmaus, and many more. From this it is easily understood why at first Luke was thought to be actually a painter. Theodore the Lector (d. 330) first mentions this (*Church History*, II, 43).

Through Nicephorus Callistus the fourteenth century brings us the Jerusalemic legend that the Empress Eudokia had in her possession an "icon" of the holy virgin painted by Luke. Unfortunately that is only a pious legend. Augustine, who was familiar with Palestine, writes in the fourth century: "We do not know what the Virgin Mary looked like" (*De Trinitate*,

VIII, 5-7). But we know Mary's language: Luke 1 and 2 show in a vivid way the "pictorial" ability of their author.

Luke is also a very sensitive and authoritative historian. Ernest Renan called the gospel of Luke "the most beautiful book in the world,"[14] and indeed it was not friendship that made him say that. Technicians praise Luke's exact descriptions. Although he was a physician and not a shipbuilder or a sailor, experts say that he was nevertheless capable of furnishing one of the best descriptions of a ship and of a sea voyage in the ancient world. Jurists commend his factual presentation of Roman legal practices. Luke had that gift of the professional historian which lets the sources speak for themselves without his intrusion. The matchless first and second chapters of Luke reveal this gift in their faithful rendering of Mary's words. Here the holy virgin herself speaks, and it is no wonder that these two chapters in their beauty are especially suited to awaken in the whole world a genuine feeling for Christmas.

Matthew in his gospel appears to us as a systematic narrator. To this quality we owe our knowledge of several speeches of Jesus which Mark had not written down, besides faithful reporting of the Jewish milieu and of the connection between the Old and New Testaments. In these respects he excels Luke. Matthew is a Palestinian and apparently knows the "dynastic circles" in Jerusalem very well. With him the "Joseph tradition" occupies the foreground (in Luke 2, the "Mary tradition"). That is to say, his account is very cautious; the Messias in his youth is portrayed as completely passive, and subject to his parents and their watchful love; his presence awakens unrest; Herod and the conditions in his realm are important, also the death of the innocent children; the Messias meets with indifference and hatred on almost every hand; he must be brought to safety; the early history in Matthew has a somewhat melancholy tone and already hints at Jesus'

14. "C'est le plus beau livre qu'il y ait." *Les Evangiles*, 1877, p. 283.

rejection by his own people, whereas Luke's account bears within it a glow of optimism and gladness of heart, as these qualities characterize the "handmaid of the Lord."

In order to understand why Matthew cites his many passages from the Old Testament so "freely" and so at variance with the Hebrew as well as the Septuagint text,[15] we must examine the language situation of his time. The Old Testament was still read aloud in Hebrew as before, but this language was so little understood by the people that in the synagogue a methurgeman (dragoman), i.e., an "interpreter," was necessary to render the reading intelligible to the congregation. In Jesus' day it was not yet permitted to write down translations; later, however, this was done, and the so-called "Targumim" [translations from Hebrew to Aramaic] came into being. In Jesus' time everyone "targumed" after his own fashion. Matthew was used to these Targum translations from boyhood up and was also familiar with the fact that every methurgeman "targumed" in his own way, so that the faithful Jew must have felt himself rather at liberty in this respect.

In spite of—or even because of—the differing emphases in both gospels, the obvious harmony of the accounts in Matthew and Luke confirms their authenticity so much the more strikingly.

Now in those days Mary arose and went with haste into the hill country, to a town of Juda. And she entered the house of Zachary and saluted Elizabeth. And it came to pass, when Elizabeth heard the greeting of Mary, that the babe in her womb leapt. And Elizabeth was filled with the Holy Spirit, and cried out with a loud voice, saying, "Blessed art thou among women and blessed is the fruit of thy womb! And how have I deserved that the mother of my Lord should come to me? For behold, the moment that the sound of thy greeting came to my ears, the

15. Septuagint: the Greek translation of the Old Testament by the so-called seventy scholars; generally abbreviated by LXX.

babe in my womb leapt for joy. And blessed is she who has believed, because the things promised her by the Lord shall be accomplished."

Luke 1:39–45

Mary behaves differently from Zacharias. The latter doubts what he hears and requires a sign; he is struck dumb until John is born. Mary however accepts the words given to her even though they do not accord with her thoughts and ideals, and says: "Behold the handmaid of the Lord; be it unto me according to thy word," and although she does not ask for a sign, one is given her: "and, behold, thy cousin Elizabeth, she hath also conceived . . ."

These words cause Mary to go to Elizabeth, but certainly not to resolve any doubts. That is not her way. She goes thankful for the angel's message, to unite her joy with Elizabeth's, and in this way to experience her own secret symbolically and in advance, so to speak. The journey took her to a city in the mountains of Judah. The place is not mentioned, but an old tradition names Ain Karim, a town about four miles west of Jerusalem. To be sure, other places are mentioned, too. Lagrange[16] lists Bethzacharia, Haran ech-Charif, and Tell Zakaria, but there is the question of whether the prophet Zachariah is not meant. Ain Karim is the best attested locale. It lies a little over six miles from Bethlehem, so Mary can have used the opportunity to join others for the trip.

However, as we learn from Matthew 1:18–20, Joseph had not yet learned of her secret at that time. He seems not to have learned of it until much later, after Mary had returned from Judea. This is not to imply that she did not trust Joseph, or that she might have been afraid to tell him. Such motives would completely contradict Joseph's and Mary's conduct. Her temporary silence had a different reason. She, the handmaid of the Lord, had

16. Lagrange, *Evangile* (Luc), p. 40 f.

received her future from heaven, and so left it in heaven's hands
as to how, when, and where Joseph would be apprised of the
mystery. It was a matter for God, not for her, and so she remained
silent. And Joseph did not accompany her to see Elizabeth; we
get the definite impression from her meeting with Elizabeth that
Joseph was not there. If he had accompanied her to Judea, his
presence would have at least been mentioned.

But to have made that kind of a trip (three to four days) in
those times, all by herself, would have been too dangerous for
Mary. Perhaps an opportunity presented itself for the journey—
caravans passing through Nazareth to Judea were common—
and once her decision to go had ripened, she went. The firmness
of resolve and independence with which she carried out her plan
is striking. She was young, but not a child. She knew what she
wanted to do, and she did it.

It was not necessary for Mary to tell Elizabeth of her secret.
Filled with the Holy Spirit, Elizabeth jubilantly greets Mary
with inspired words (Lk 1:41). She speaks as a prophetess; even
before Mary has spoken she knows that her cousin has experienced
a revelation and that its meaning has already become a reality
for and within her.

The actions of the angel Gabriel and of Elizabeth form a very
vital and strong beginning—even proof—of the church's veneration for Mary; the visitation of the angel and Elizabeth's salutation
are the source and keynote of its later development.

And when Elizabeth greeted her relative with such abundant
and inspired joy, it would have been surprising if Mary had not
been moved to reply in kind. Mary's answer is more than just
an echo of Elizabeth's salutation—it is a psalm expressing in rich
tones her confession of faith.

> And Mary said, "My soul magnifies the Lord, and my spirit
> rejoices in God my Savior; Because he has regarded the lowliness
> of his handmaid; for, behold, henceforth all generations shall call

me blessed; Because he who is mighty has done great things for me, and holy is his name; And for generation upon generation is his mercy, to those who fear him. He has shown might with his arm, he has scattered the proud in the conceit of their heart. He has put down the mighty from their thrones, and has exalted the lowly. He has filled the hungry with good things, and the rich he has sent away empty. He has given help to Israel, his servant, mindful of his mercy—Even as he spoke to our fathers—to Abraham and to his posterity forever."

Luke 1: 46–55

Here we have the glorious *Magnificat*, heart and soul of the holy maid, the basis and center of all Christmas feeling. The name *Magnificat* is taken from the first word of the Latin translation. The song is strongly reminiscent of the Old Testament; words from the latter echo and re-echo in it. It is a living illustration of the theological words: *Novum testamentum in vetere latet, vetus testamentum in novo patet*, that is, the New Testament lies hidden in the Old, the Old Testament reveals itself in the New.

Elizabeth honored the mother of her God when she visited her; Mary brings to God all honor. Her song is the antiphonal morning psalmody for the breaking of the messianic day; the words still belong to the Old Testament, the tones to the New— their keynote is grace. Every thought in the *Magnificat* is of an Old Testament mode, yet every word is bathed in the golden light of the new day. And this golden light is the life, death, and resurrection of Jesus Christ. This psalm could not have been spoken either by the Jews or by the pagans. Despite its Old Testament borrowings, it is in its delivery and train of thought original, and the expression of a genuine experience. It is evident, too, that Mary was not merely a "pious maiden." This psalm reveals a heart completely at home in the depths of the Old Testament, and one which in its youthful freshness can lend its own accent to those depths. Here a great soul in God's kingdom begins the liturgy of the Christmas event. "Mary arises in the

Magnificat as a great figure. God sends her a message, and she receives it like one of the great of Israel. She is a singing prophetess like the ancestral women of her people, like Mariam, the sister of Moses (Ex 15:20 f.), like Debbora (Jg 5), and Judith (Jud 16). She takes her place beside the great men and women whose fame is on everyone's lips, and she knows herself to be exalted above them as the mother of the Messias. In the theology of the Church Fathers Mary is therefore called a prophetess. The Church's veneration for her has raised her title even higher to that of queen of the prophets."[17]

> And Mary remained with her about three months and returned to her own house.
>
> Luke 1:56

Since Mary received the annunciation when Elizabeth had been with child six months, the latter's time would be fulfilled in three months. Mary could have stayed these three months with Elizabeth and then departed shortly before Elizabeth gave birth; this is the conventional interpretation because of the sequence of the scriptural texts. But the text, on the other hand, does not rule out the possibility of Mary's having remained until after Elizabeth's delivery. Psychologically viewed, it seems rather obvious that she would. That she would remain three months seems to indicate she wanted also to see the precursor of Jesus. This is in fact quite understandable in view of the angel's words to Mary that Elizabeth's son would be a sign to her. Moreover, it makes sense to assume that a relative who came to visit three months before the birth of a child and stayed that long would also want to be present for the event itself—especially under the circumstances surrounding this one.

It should be noted that in Israel an unmarried girl was not

17. Schelkle, p. 77.

permitted to be present at a birth; but as a betrothed person Mary had more freedom according to Jewish law, and if even so her "presence" would not have been proper, she could have waited in the vicinity. It seems quite natural and very probable that she would want to see the child before undertaking the long return journey. However, she could hardly have stayed until the circumcision of John eight days later; that she is no longer present, and even intended not to be, is evident in the manner of the narration. We may assume she departed some time between the birth of John and the circumcision. This is the opinion also of many Latin Church Fathers.

Did Joseph come to take her back? Apparently not; more probably she again found facilities for the return journey. In any event the solemnization of her marriage to Joseph occurred after her return, which seems to rule out Joseph's fetching her from Judea.

At the end of the text reporting the feast of the circumcision in the house of Zacharias and Elizabeth, we read :

> And fear came on all their neighbors; and all these things were spoken abroad in all the hill country of Judea.
>
> Luke 1:65

Since the birth of John precedes that of Jesus by half a year, the news of it was probably reinforced by that from Bethlehem—in Judea reports of a Messias found general acceptance and awakened hopes for the future. Whether or not people remembered this thirty years later, when John preached, and after him Jesus, is not told us; but they very likely often did remember.

The allusions in Luke 1:5–23 to the priestly office of Zacharias often have served as a point of departure in the attempt to calculate the years of Jesus' birth. Zacharias received the angel's message in the temple in Jerusalem where he was discharging his priestly office. Even in David's time the priests were divided into twenty-four orders (1 Chr 24:3–19), and under Solomon were charged with certain fixed duties (2 Chr 23:8; cf. 5:11). The first order was that of Jojarib, the eighth that of Abia, to which Zacharias belonged. Flavius Josephus, who, as he himself says, belonged to the order of Jojarib, mentions that even in his time these twenty-four orders still regularly attended to their duties, each order for one week; the service of each order would begin on a Saturday morning.

Now according to 1 Maccabees 4:52 the sacrifices in the temple had been discontinued for three years under Antiochus Epiphanes, but were restored on the twenty-fifth day of the ninth month Kaslev in the year 148 of the Greeks (i.e., of the Selucidian era). Supposedly they began again with the first order of Jojarib; the eighth order of Abia would follow seven weeks after the starting time of the first order. We can also reckon on the basis of the old Jewish tradition, that in the year 70 at the destruction of the temple the first order of Jojarib was performing its office, namely, on the ninth day of the month Ab.

These two modes of calculation, however, do not yield unequivocal results, and furthermore contain too many possibilities of erroneous interpretation to allow much certainty here. For one thing, we cannot prove that the restoration of priestly service under the Maccabees started with the first order. For another, it is only a tradition (which, like others, could be false) that the first order of Jojarib was officiating at the time of the temple's destruction. We further do not know whether or not during the centuries there were changes in the sequence or service for the various orders.

In view of these uncertainties and all the problems stemming from the many chronologies, we cannot assess the otherwise interesting calculation of the time of Zacharias' service in the temple and his hearing of the angel's message. It is today generally agreed that all these calculations are without foundation.[18] Let us return with Mary to Nazareth! Matthew says:

> Now the origin of Christ was in this wise. When Mary his mother had been betrothed to Joseph, she was found, before they came together, to be with child by the Holy Spirit. But Joseph her husband, being a just man, and not wishing to expose her to reproach, was minded to put her away privately. But while he thought on these things, behold, an angel of the Lord appeared to him in a dream, saying, "Do not be afraid, Joseph, son of David, to take to thee Mary thy wife, for that which is begotten in her is of the Holy Spirit. And she shall bring forth a son, and thou shalt call his name Jesus; for he shall save his people from their sins." Now all this came to pass that there might be fulfilled what was spoken by the Lord through the prophet, saying, "Behold, the virgin shall be with child, and shall bring forth a son; and they shall call his name Emmanuel"; which is, interpreted, "God with us." So Joseph, arising from sleep, did as the Angel of the Lord had commanded him, and took unto him his wife. And he did not know her till she had brought forth her firstborn son. And he called his name Jesus.
>
> Matthew 1:18–25

We see that Matthew's account omits any reference to the annunciation to Mary and her visit to Elizabeth. Yet he does not actually exclude these events, but rather tacitly assumes that the announcement to Mary, which removed any astonishment she may have had at her pregnancy, has already taken place; for Mary does not appear here in any way uncertain or surprised, as if confronted with a riddle. No, what Joseph now hears in Matthew 1:20 she already knows, as the text supposes, and her knowledge must have accorded with what Joseph now learns. She has "conceived . . . of the Holy Spirit." Matthew assumes Mary knows this, and it follows from this assumption that Matthew

---

18. Lagrange says rightly: "On avoue aujourd'hui que tous ces calculs manquent de bases," (*Evangile*, on Luke 1:6).

as well as Luke teaches the virgin birth. There was no doubt among the evangelists on this point.

This is not contradicted by Matthew's reference to Joseph as "her husband" and to Mary as "his wife," for in the same breath he speaks also of the "espoused" and thereby confirms the Jewish custom of referring to "man" and "wife" right after their betrothal, or engagement.

We see also from Matthew's account that Mary does not impart her secret to Joseph even after her return from Judea, but continues in her attitude of waiting silence. This was made easier for her by her three months' visit with Elizabeth. In Nazareth it would not have been easy to conceal from Joseph this profound event concerning them. But even after her return she is silent and waits. The motive is clear. She waits to see if God, who was mindful of Elizabeth and of her, will likewise be mindful of him who is to be the legal father of the child. Joseph is no secondary person in these events and must not be so considered. Mary fully recognizes him as a father. If the angel summons her, he will also summon the father; she is only the handmaid of the Lord. She waits to see how God will make this known to Joseph; the *Lord* will give the holy child not only a mother, but also a father. This is the paternal honor which Mary in her silence ascribes to Joseph with great respect and a deep religious sense. Subsequent events prove her right.

However, it must have been difficult for Joseph when he learns of her pregnancy upon her return. We don't know whether he learned from others or by directly questioning Mary. We only know that Mary kept to her resolve not to give any explanation on her own.

What a situation for Joseph! He had offered Mary his support with the purpose of protecting this high-minded girl and her vow of virginity, a situation which doubtless brought her social ostracism and even hostility. And now she expects a child, fathered by a stranger, and declines to give him an explanation. What man, however understanding, would not lose his self-control in such circumstances! Perhaps the villagers in Nazareth mockingly asked him about the ostensibly pious and religious girl he had taken under his care. Joseph was mature and thoughtful, but this was not to be borne. But he would not expose her, i.e., officially divorce her, as was often customary in such cases. He would "put her away" secretly. That this secrecy could only be partial— the breaking off of the betrothal and the reason for it could not remain a secret forever—was of course clear to him; he nevertheless chose the way that would be the easiest on Mary.

If Mary surmised any of Joseph's thoughts, we are not told about it; it is quite possible that she did, and she certainly could understand how he must have felt. But despite the danger for her she left the solution of all this to heaven; she knew that the angel had said: The *Lord God* will give him the throne of his father David. How that would come about was God's affair. She had great faith! And then occurred what Mary had hoped for and awaited. The angel comes to Joseph and speaks also to him of the inheritance of David's throne. The angel speaks with him in a dream and addresses him like a friend. He calls him David's son—except in the genealogical accounts this is the only passage in which someone other than Jesus is accorded this title of honor, and we become attentive.

The angel uses this address with clear intent. Joseph has been tormenting himself with the question of Mary's pregnancy; his anguish is the greater when Mary remains silent. But he is now called "the son of David"! Would not the "Old Testament" Joseph at this manner of address immediately think of the messianic promises of the house of David—promises which indeed spoke of a wonderful child? This child comes to the son of David from the Holy Spirit! To this son of David the words are clear—they mean: *Messias*. And so Joseph understands them;

he could not interpret them differently. The angel has told him something that no writer had imagined; just one sentence, but this sentence reveals the greatest of all secrets: God's spirit has conceived the child!

Joseph now understands Mary, and understands how it is that the devout girl has been chosen by God to become the mother of the Messias promised to his line. The child is conceived of the Holy Spirit, and these words with all their mystery somehow sound familiar; at least they are founded, like the inscrutable words of God uttered by the ancient prophets, on an allusion to the future.

The son of David, says the angel. We can understand the great love for Mary that would ascribe to her everything possible, even a Davidian ancestry, but the angelic message says that the sonship of David for the child to come will pass to him through Joseph. The impression created by the text in Matthew is clear. To find a Davidian ancestry for Mary is to miss the real content of the text. Joseph is also to name the child, and with this it is expressed anew that the future child is related to the line of David through Joseph, and that at the same time Joseph is personally designated as the chosen father—with all the rights and duties of a father.

The one to come is to be called Jesus. For the Greeks as well as for us the name needed an explanation (Jesus, or Josua, or "Jahve is salvation"); to Hebraic ears, and therefore to Joseph, the name was immediately comprehensible. When the multitude shouted "Hosianna" at the entry of Jesus into Jerusalem, the same Hebrew word found expression: Hail, salvation from Jahve! Messias!

It is noteworthy that the Jews had sought in prechristian times to guess what the name of the Messias would be, and made a number of proposals; the name Jesus was not among them. The rabbinical suggestions were: Yinnon, Adonai, the Just One,

Tsemach, Menachen, David, Shiloh, Elijah, Anani, Chaninah (thus Midrasch on Proverbs 19:21).[19]

Joseph acted, as did the patriarchs when God spoke, and acted quickly. He was a man of mature, but quick decision. We are told that as soon as he awoke from his sleep, he did as the angel had bade him, and took Mary to wife. Not much time seems to have elapsed, nor would he have dared wait much longer, for others could have learned that Mary was with child. The people in whose company Mary had returned from "Ain Karim" could have heard of Elizabeth's and Zacharias' loud rejoicing and have told of it in Nazareth, the more so, since no secret was made of what happened there and in the vicinity; perhaps word of it had spread throughout the hills of Judea. Moreover, merchant caravans plied continually between Judea and Galilee, and Nazareth was on their route. It would have been indeed strange if these things were not known in Nazareth. The contrary is far more probable, and Mary from then on needed secure protection. Joseph knew that, and accordingly moved swiftly. The expression "took unto him his wife" is the Jewish expression for legal marriage. That Mary then told Joseph all that she and Elizabeth had experienced, is very probable. Joseph now had a right to hear of those matters.

Not much time could have elapsed between the legal marriage and the journey to Bethlehem. Mary was in her fourth month at this time, and Joseph and Mary knew quite well that they could not choose the final months for the long journey.[20]

Naturally Joseph and Mary are legally married when they both set out for Bethlehem, and Jesus was not born of an unmarried woman as an "illegitimate" child. And when in Luke 2:5 we read ". . . to be taxed with Mary his espoused wife, being great with child," the Evangelist wants to emphasize with

19. Cf. W. Michaelis, *Das Evangelium nach Matthäus*, 1948, p. 59.
20. Cf. P. Gaechter, *Maria im Erdenleben*, 2nd ed. 1954, pp. 78–126.

this consciously chosen expression the fact, known to him and to all, that the couple had had no sexual relations although legally married (apart from the question of whether the translator fully captures the Greek original with the word "espoused"; the Vulgate is here at variance: *cum desponsata sibi uxore*, "with the wife pledged to him"). On the other hand, we must not over-interpret the words and intent of Luke, which is what happens when we often hear in Christmas narratives of the "betrothed" Mary. Youth has little understanding for this, and is justifiably critical of such interpretations. Unfortunately, their criticism is then directed not against the narrator, but against the sanctity and authenticity of the event itself.

"And Joseph knew her not till she had brought forth her firstborn son," says Matthew. These words do not imply that Joseph subsequently had sexual relations with Mary, any more than the words from 2 Samuel 6:23: "Michal the daughter of Saul had no child unto the day of her death," imply that she bore a child after that. The expression is a Jewish idiom expressing simply that Joseph "knew her not," and no more.

> Now all this came to pass that there might be fulfilled what was spoken by the Lord through the prophet, saying, "Behold, the virgin shall be with child, and shall bring forth a son; . . ."
>
> Matthew 1:22 f.

Whoever maintains that the virgin birth has been invented to fulfill the prophecy of Isaiah, forgets that the Jewish schools have never interpreted these words of Isaiah in this way. On the contrary, the Jewish schools assert repeatedly that indeed the prophets were infallible, but that Isaiah did err once: When in Isaiah 7:14 he spoke of an "almah" who was to give birth, he should have used the word—so they think—"almunah" (young woman). In explaining this passage no scholar of the Jewish schools has ever meant what the angel told to Joseph as a fact. The accuracy of the language of the Isaiah passage is thus only reinforced. It becomes clear from this that the prophecy contains more than humans could ever devise, and that Isaiah, doubtless saying more than he himself knew or could know, thus prophesied with the word "almah" the virgin birth of Jesus. "For we have not followed cunningly devised fables, when we made known unto you the power and coming of our Lord Jesus Christ" (2 Pt 1:16).

CHAPTER III

THE STABLE

WHEN JOSEPH and Mary arrived in Bethlehem they learned that the lodgings in the village were already pretty well filled. Many who, like Joseph, wanted to protect their interests in the registration had already arrived. Now it is understandable that the hot sub-tropical summer of Jesus' birth has been magically transformed by the popular mind (especially in Christmas plays) into a cold Germanic winter, even though there are no grounds for such a change; this reversal of seasons is fine for Europe, if not for Bethlehem.

But it is crude nonsense to portray Joseph as a poor simpleton who helplessly stumbles along behind his wife, and stands by with an expressionless countenance which seems only to say (if it says anything): "I simply can't do anything about this situation." It is equally silly to portray cruel Bethlehemites who have no feeling at all for the young woman, and to show Joseph and Mary as having found lodging with an ox and an ass in a place where the birth of the Savior would take place under morally and physically impossible circumstances.

Poor Joseph! He plays the role in Christmas plays of a harmless supernumerary, who was unable to provide Mary with decent lodging. Often one has the impression that he is there only because he has no place else to go; when he speaks, he speaks despite his helplessness with fatherly mien and utters to Mary (who of course listens to him with angelic patience) a few commonplaces that only show he must say *something*. The only genuine impression we get of Joseph is the sight of the large staff he carries in his hand; the staff indicated a long journey, and in reality he had taken a long journey—but is there anything else of meaning? Is this, then, the saintly Joseph whom God gave as protector to Mary, full of grace, and in whom she might place her complete trust?

We should venerate our saints! In his native town of Bethlehem, where honor would be given to one of David, the highly respected Joseph was surely not surrounded by "cruel" Bethlehemites—quite the opposite, for here he found every assistance and support he could wish for. On the strength of that alone it is certain that Joseph, if he didn't find lodging with his relatives or would accept none from them, would still obtain quarters that would be satisfactory to most and certainly to him as the responsible protector of the Holy Family. It would of course not have been a palace, nor would the carpenter wish for such, but a decent lodging. This should be clarified somewhat.

First of all, the birth took place in the full sub-tropical summer of Judea. The changing of Christmas day to the end of the year in the European winter didn't take place till many centuries later, for reasons we will examine subsequently. For now, let us fix the birth at a time when the shepherds were out in the fields. They were there—and the Talmud confirms it for us—from Passover to the beginning of the rainy season, about the beginning of November. During this period the sheds of the caravansary were available to guests.

These stables must be visualized as round enclosures surrounded by a broad, rough wall. Their covering, or roof, sloped toward a common center, an opening above a basin to collect the rain water; the entire structure was not quite circular in form. Bethlehem was and is today in the mountains of Judea, which are from about 2,000 to almost 2,700 feet high. The owner of the caravansary could easily have incorporated caves or grottoes into his stables, and then rented them. Thus the traditional grotto birthplace could have been a part of the stables. Such a stable, with many partitions, forms the background of the parable of the Good Shepherd; the shepherd calls his own sheep, they know his voice and come. Here we must picture the stall described above, where each shepherd rents his own section or partition, calls his sheep and leads them in and out through the main door.

For the flocks, grass was the most important thing. In the summer the fields would become brown and barren, making it necessary for the herdsmen to take their flocks far up into the mountains to find pasture. Under these conditions it was not possible to return home at night, nor was it necessary, for in sub-tropical regions one can easily spend the night in the open fields; moreover, in this way the herders saved rental expenses for the stalls. But with the rainy season the shepherds came back, and this would last from about the beginning of November to Easter. In winter, i.e., in the rainy season, grass was in abundance nearby, and it was then better for sheep and shepherds to have shelter. The poorer shepherds, who had no stall of their own, would rent a section of the caravansary, and so the flocks would remain in the stalls only during this time of year.

In summer these stables were completely empty and provided good living quarters. They might have been just as good as any room in the village. "There was no room for them in the inn," says the text very simply. This calm and clear statement should not be elaborately dramatized. The room in the stables was probably very little different from the rooms in the inn and in summer was perhaps even pleasanter. And Joseph would have been a bad carpenter if he couldn't have made the necessary repairs and alterations. We can imagine that he was glad to find a grotto in one of the sections of the stable, for the temperature would certainly be more comfortable there in the summer, and the room perhaps more spacious. There is no reason to reject the idea of a grotto, for Joseph had plenty of friends and relatives in Bethlehem who would help him if it were necessary to make a stable or grotto inhabitable. Even though it was a stable in which the King of Kings was born, there need be no talk here of dire misery.

Joseph and Mary would live here for several months; they knew that in advance. In order to spare Mary, Joseph set out on the trip from Nazareth as soon as possible, probably even *before* Passover. Luke 2:22 shows that they remained in Bethlehem for forty days after Jesus' birth. Since presumably the rainy season had not yet begun, we can infer that they stayed on there until fall.

> And it came to pass while they were there, that the days for her to be delivered were fulfilled. And she brought forth her firstborn son, and wrapped him in swaddling clothes, and laid him in a manger, because there was no room for them in the inn.
>
> Luke 2:6–7

The great event is very simply told. The words breathe the spirit of Mary, the handmaid of the Lord. That she laid her child in a crib, or manger, does not mean that this crib was filled with harsh straw, as is often portrayed in pictures. There had to be a crib in every stable. This was adaptable as a bed for the child; we do Joseph and his relatives an injustice to think that this crib was made less comfortable than was customary in such places. There was ample time to make it ready. Too poor? Joseph was, as noted, a man of the middle class; he certainly would not go on a trip without money. He had his friends and relatives in Bethlehem. Anyway, who would imagine he spent all his time there without working? Would any man calmly sit around for several months without doing any work? And more, could he have taken this attitude as provider for the holy child and his mother?

Again, we would do Joseph great wrong to say he played the role of protector without really protecting. The Christmas romantics may be fond of painting in stark colors, but they are not aware that they make an irresponsible fumbler out of a capable and righteous man, whose sanctity is beyond question. The Christmas narrators mean well, but must be taught better. They must not insult their saints even if it happens unintentionally. Mary had a husband, and the Christ child a father, to whom we must not impute outrageous things.

Joseph was a carpenter in Nazareth, and in his workshop Jesus no doubt learned the carpenter's trade. Is it right to assume from the very outset that manual workers are "poor"? Today, certainly, such is not the case, but even in Jesus' time those who worked with their hands were by no means "poor people"! Or will it perhaps be said that Joseph was poor because unemployed? Such nonsense is easily refuted: In the kingdom of Herod a great deal of construction was going on, in fact Herod was known for his mania for building, and was responsible for the creation of entire cities. Given this situation, a poor or out of work carpenter was either lazy or a ne'er-do-well. Certainly no one would maintain this of Joseph, whose work would have to serve as a model for the boy Jesus? With representations such as these, people do not recognize, nay, they insult the greatness of Joseph, and with him the entire Holy Family.

It is also a foolish thing whenever the Christmas narrators in our northern lands cry, in moving tones: the little babe had no clothing; Mary had only strips of cloth in which to wrap the child. Clothing? As if people in Palestine at that time or even today forced children into northern European clothing in the hot summer! The children lay mostly naked in their beds. And if Mary wrapped her son in swaddling clothes, it was a sign of respect.

It is likewise silly to imagine the crib and Jesus' birth in the midst of cattle. That would have been a disgrace both for Joseph and for Bethlehem. Of course there were no cattle here, for the stable (and grotto) were vacant in the summertime. The birth of Jesus took place at the end of August, as we will later show. That people in later times pictured an ox and an ass near the crib, was not meant to be historical. In so doing they were thinking of Isaiah 1:3: "The ox knoweth his owner, and the ass his master's crib," and intended to portray *allegorically* the fulfillment of this prophecy at the crib in Bethlehem. A crib is mentioned in Isaiah 1:3, but whether the crib in Bethlehem is meant is at least open to question; in any case this medieval allegory didn't mean that ox and ass really stood near the crib in Bethlehem. A literal understanding of the allegory may still have been possible in the Middle Ages, but oughtn't we to reject it? If ox and ass are represented in Christmas stables today, it is to be hoped that children are sufficiently instructed in the allegorical sense of what they see.

This allegory is further strengthened by an apparently false translation of Habakkuk 3:2 in the Septuagint: "In the midst of two animals thou art revealed." In the Hebrew text animals are not mentioned at all; rather, we have: "In the midst of the years thou art revealed." There were sheep in Bethlehem; we don't know if there were oxen. There were probably some mules; in any case Joseph brought one along. He might have kept this animal for the return trip, or perhaps he used it in the flight to Egypt. A stall would easily have been found for it, in any event, but naturally not in the same room the family stayed in.

It is an important question, and a matter of principle, as to whether we might not do better to do away with the traditional Christmas stables as having had their day. They blended harmoniously into medieval art, and they had something to say to the people of that time; in our century they only cause difficulty.

They suggest a reality that was no reality, and thus undermine faith. Whoever doesn't detect this does not know our age. If it is objected that art be allowed to go its own way, then we fully agree, but it is certain in any event that art in the twentieth century must reflect the twentieth century, and that the Church cannot be content with an art that was timely a thousand years ago. Naturally, a Christmas art is quite desirable: the beautiful feast surrounding the Holy Family with song and music ought to be celebrated with the most beautiful works of art that man can devise, but not with an art that is weighed down with the inertia of the past. Rather, it must be inspired anew. We may say, along with Hermann Baur: "The world in transformation, the coming new world expects from the Church something bold and strong. Staying obstinately on the same well-worn track, be it out of ignorance, expediency, or mere comfortableness, does not lead anywhere but into the lukewarmness that God spews out of his mouth. Only a Christian art that is as daring and strikingly new as the day of creation will be able to penetrate the soul of modern man and reach it."[1] If the well-known Swiss architect is correct in this impassioned statement, which he made in 1957 in a lecture on the occasion of the Second World Congress of the Lay Apostolate in Rome, then we must hope that the false romanticism of the medieval Christmas stable, so foreign to the gospels—a romanticism which no longer has a message for moderns—will soon come to an end or be replaced by a Christian art which will be in keeping with the twentieth century.

And there were shepherds in the same district living in the fields and keeping watch over their flock by night. And behold, an angel of the Lord stood by them and the glory of God shone

1. H. Baur, *Il mondo attende la chiesa*, Editrice Studium, 1958, p. 149. (German edition: *Katholiken sprechen zur Welt*, ed. by Weltsekretariat f. d. Laienapostolat, 1958.)

round about them, and they feared exceedingly. And the angel said to them, "Do not be afraid, for behold, I bring you good news of great joy which shall be to all the people; for there has been born to you today in the town of David a Savior, who is Christ the Lord. And this shall be a sign to you: you will find an infant wrapped in swaddling clothes and lying in a manger." And suddenly there was with the angel a multitude of the heavenly host praising God and saying, "Glory to God in the highest, and peace on earth among men of good will." And it came to pass, when the angels had departed from them into heaven, that the shepherds were saying to one another, "Let us go over to Bethlehem and see this thing that has come to pass, which the Lord has made known to us." So they went with haste, and they found Mary and Joseph, and the babe lying in the manger. And when they had seen, they understood what had been told them concerning this child. And all who heard marvelled at the things told them by the shepherds. But Mary kept in mind all these words, pondering them in her heart. And the shepherds returned, glorifying and praising God for all that they had heard and seen, even as it was spoken to them.

Luke 2:8–20

In this account it becomes clear to us that the *real* beauty surrounding the Christmas event puts all the false romanticizing pathos concerning it in the shade.

As in Luke 1:19, the angel uses the word *euangelizomai*, i.e., "I bring you tidings of great joy." Here occurs the first evangelic announcement of the New Testament, the beginning of the "great joy" which it is the task and commission of Christ's Church to impart until the end of the world.

The announcement is to the shepherds. Nothing is known of them except for their mention in Luke 2. We know, however, that the ancient Jewish promises of the faith were very often discussed among shepherds. In history, shepherds have always been a prototype of pious wisdom. Their peaceful life with nature and with the animals, and their solicitude, faithfulness, and providence during the watches brought forth virtues hardly developed in the frenetic pace of city life. In Israel, at the nightly watch-fires of the shepherds, the fate and the hope of that occupied country were passionately discussed and suffered through more than in Jerusalem. The urban collaborators hated shepherds. But it was first to these very shepherds that the angel of God announced the Good Tidings, of which the entire world would later be aware.

It is worthy of note that Bethlehem, the birth of the Messias there, and the shepherds of Bethlehem had always played a prominent role in Jewish literature. Bethlehem was named in the Old Testament prophecies as the birthplace of the Messias, and the Jews actually expected his birth in that very place. We hear of this quite plainly when Herod interrogates the Sanhedrin for his information.

But the shepherds of Bethlehem also play a part in the ancient expectations. We know this from the Targumim. The Targums, i.e., scriptural explanations, interpreted in Aramaic the scripture readings for the ordinary people who after the Exile knew insufficient Hebrew. The best known Targums stem from the rabbis Onkelos and Jonathan the son of Uzziel, usually abbreviated as Targum pseud. Jon., because Jonathan was only an assumed name. The Targum pseud. Jon. mentions, concerning Genesis 35:21, that the Migdal Eder, i.e., the watch tower of the shepherds at Bethlehem, was the tower from which the birth of the Messias was to be announced. In the text of Luke's gospel no tower is mentioned; nevertheless it is not impossible that the shepherds in the field who "were keeping watch over their flock by night" held this night watch in or near their Migdal Eder, their watch tower. This mention of the tower in those ancient Targums says, in effect: The shepherds are like heralds, who proclaim their joy to the land.

Another Jewish collection, the Mishna (Shek. 7, 4), states that right in the vicinity of Bethlehem the temple flocks grazed, i.e., the sheep marked for sacrifice in the temple. Their shepherds were closely connected with the temple, and they were in part under direct control of the priests, and in part the priests bought the sheep from them. According to old Jewish belief these shepherds of the temple flocks were to be the first heralds announcing the coming of the Messias.

The miraculous fulfillment of this Jewish folk belief was now at hand, and this was clear to the shepherds in Bethlehem. For the beliefs concerning Bethlehem were certainly well known to them and often were subject of conversations at the watch fires. If their flocks were specially designated for sacrifice as "temple flocks"—it was a two hour journey on foot from Bethlehem to Jerusalem—then their "proclamation" was heard of not only in the mountains of Juda, but surely in the temple as well. Perhaps Simeon learned in this way of the events in Bethlehem; he and the shepherds had been acquainted for many years.

The song of the angels is strongly reminiscent of the temple cult. When in the temple the sacrifice had been laid on the altar, the temple music would begin three times, each time introduced by a priest sounding a silver trumpet. This was the "Tris-Hagion" (thrice-holy). According to Jewish tradition the three blasts on the trumpet denoted (1) the Kingdom of God, (2) God's providence, and (3) God's final judgment. Likewise the announcement to the shepherds was accomplished in three phases, as in the temple:

> Glory to God in the highest
> and peace on earth to
> men of good will!

These three phases are not dissimilar to the message of the temple music. But this music is richer and more beautiful than any the shepherds could ever hear in the temple. The Tris-Hagion of the angels, in the holy temple of the night that enveloped the child in its crib, forms the first "Christmas mass"![2]

The angel said that they would find the child "lying in a manger." This sign was quite sufficient, for that could only be in the stables now being used as living quarters, as these shepherds very well knew. They knew equally well that in these quarters Joseph of the house of David was living, together with his young wife, who was with child. Their first thought would be right away: Joseph and his wife! The house of David!—Could this really be the fulfillment? The angel mentioned no other name than that of David, nor did he have to, for the shepherds understood him. The sign was made very clear to them: a child, wrapped in swaddling clothes, lying in a manger. The great light that had shown upon them in the night seems also to have illumined their minds. They left in great haste to see and to be convinced of what they had heard. They did not ask where they were to go, for there was no uncertainty about this: naturally they would go to the stables and to the room where Joseph and his wife were staying.

They found Mary, Joseph, and the child that lay in the manger. What words must have been exchanged during that night by the crib! The shepherds had come as children of God, sent by an angel of God to Mary and Joseph. They were permitted to learn what a miracle God had performed with Joseph and Mary. In that moment the hearts of the shepherds must have been illumined, and they must have been inspired when they heard what had happened there.

Our faith is first and foremost a great joy! Let us never forget

2. Very well-informed concerning the ancient Jewish literature is the great English-American work: A. Edersheim, *Life and Times of Jesus the Messiah*, 2 vols., which had its 36th printing in 1953. The Jewish interpretations of the Old Testament Messianic prophecies are presented here in exemplary fashion.

that. The light came into the night, and later into Bethlehem also came dark days, days of flight, of slaughter of children; and there must have been in that night a presentiment of such things. All concerned were surely aware of how things were under Herod, the Romans, and the Jewish collaborators. And yet what had begun with such gladness would surely end in the same way.

In the angels' song of praise, "Glory to God in the highest and peace on earth to men of good will," the translation "of good will," which goes back to the Latin translation, does not fully satisfy us. In what language the angels sang we do not know—was it in the Aramaic vernacular or in the more elevated religious language of the Hebrew, which the faithful, having heard it in the synagogue from their youth up, understood well enough to grasp the meaning of the angelic tidings? It is not likely that the hymn of praise was sung in Greek, the language of officials and of the educated. More probably they sang it in Hebrew, the ancient tongue of the Messianic prophecies. The Hebrew equivalent of that part of the song under discussion had grammatically an objective rather than a subjective reference. The translation "men of good will" in the sense of "men, who have good will," has subjective reference. The more correct sense of the angels' words would be: "men *tes eudokias* of God," i.e., men having the good favor of God. This interpretation finds its confirmation in the fact that the entire train of events during that wonderful night was from beginning to end the gift of God, a favor from God for which men had only to give grateful praises. It is not at all a matter here of "subjective good will." Writes Joseph Schmid: "The sense of the original text is: Because of the birth of the Messias, God is glorified in the high heavens and on earth salvation has come to men from the divine favor." He says further, "by this is not meant (as with the Vulgate) men who have good will, but rather, men who experience God's pleasure, i.e., his freely prevailing mercy and goodness."[3] Catholic exegesis therefore advocates this better translation.*

After the shepherds left the manger, they were not silent. "And all they that heard it wondered at those things which were told them by the shepherds," says the text. They may not literally have proclaimed their joy to the land from the Migdal Eder, but they must have gladly continued to tell of their experience. Much was spoken about these things in the mountains of Judea at that time. And when the Bethlehemites asked Joseph—as they naturally did—what these happenings meant, both Joseph and Mary confirmed the truth of what they had been asked about. Moreover the Bethlehemites knew very well what the prophets had said of Bethlehem. And we also know from Luke 1:59–79 what happened in the house of Zacharias. When Zacharias spoke, and expressed his thoughts joyfully in his song of praise, his neighbors were witnesses of this "proclamation." Luke tells us that "fear came on all that dwelt round about them: and all these sayings were noised abroad throughout all the hill country of Judea."

The forerunner of Jesus had seen the light of day six months earlier. In this half a year the talk concerning John that had circulated amongst the entire hill country had not yet abated; on the contrary, as the news from Bethlehem went from mouth to mouth, people recalled the earlier news from Ain Karim, and put the two together.

It must not be imagined, however, that such rumors made an alarming impression outside the circle of those directly involved.

3. Josef Schmid, *Das Evangelium nach Lukas*, 3rd ed. 1955 (on Lk 2:8–20).

*Translator's note: It is ecumenically worthy of note that the Protestant King James' version reads ". . . on earth peace, good will toward men," a translation quite in line with the author's and J. Schmid's interpretation, and incidentally, over three hundred and fifty years old. RSV has ". . . on earth peace among men with whom he is pleased!"

There were many rumors in Israel of a Messias. In the very difficult times of the Maccabees, and later of the Romans and the Herods, there was everywhere a hope stretched almost to the breaking point: Is it not yet the time? Many arose and said: I am the Messias. Earlier we noted at least six national Messias, and there were probably more. Now people heard of a new-born baby! Well, it would take a while for him to be a Messias! With all the tense expectancy of that time a rumor of this sort, although noised about, could scarcely have had an alarming effect—not even for Herod.

Nevertheless these rumors were potentially dangerous for those immediately concerned. The cautious ones had admonished: Be careful with whom you speak, and don't forget that Jerusalem is only five miles away. Probably people in Jerusalem had heard these rumors. Caution is never an attribute of the crowd, and Joseph, his friends, and his relatives knew this well enough. Their joy was mingled with a certain amount of concern, for everyone knew that Herod was bad, and in Jerusalem lived the worst Jews—people who because of money and influential position had made common cause with the enemy, and served the avaricious and power-mad Herod and the Romans. Joseph may well have walked through Bethlehem with worry and dark forebodings. "But Mary kept all these things, and pondered them in her heart." She was and continued to be the "handmaid of the Lord," who lived between heaven and her child and who relied confidently on her husband in external matters. With him, she and her child were in good hands.

We read no more, however, of the registration. It may have reached Joseph either before or after the birth and its attendant wonders, but beside that great event it sinks to the level of a mere formality. If we assume that in a small village such as Bethlehem the registration may have lasted about three months, and that Joseph arrived in an already overflowing Bethlehem shortly before or after the Passover, and that therefore upon his arrival the beginning of registration was imminent, then it is possible it was Joseph's turn to register just before Jesus' birth. However, it is to be considered that Joseph could formally register the rights of his son only when it was officially established that he had a son and not a daughter, viz., after the birth. Joseph could have validated this with the registration commission. In any event he remained in Bethlehem at least forty days after the birth of Jesus.

> And when eight days were fulfilled for his circumcision, his name was called Jesus, the name given him by the angel before he was conceived in the womb.
>
> Luke 2:21

The circumcision took place (Gn 17:12; 21:4; Lv 12:3; cf. Lk 1:59–65) in the presence of neighbors and relatives, and was a solemn occasion. The message of the shepherds and the rumors throughout Judea's hills would have made it unlikely that merely a small gathering was present at the ceremony.

According to Jewish custom this ceremony was linked with the naming of the child. Unlike the situation with Zacharias, there was no problem here. The angel had told first Mary and then Joseph that the new-born boy should receive the name Jesus (Mt 1:21).

CHAPTER IV

THE MAGI

Now when Jesus was born in Bethlehem of Judea, in the days of King Herod, behold, there came Magi from the East to Jerusalem, saying, "Where is the newly born king of the Jews? For we have seen his star in the East and have come to worship him."

Matthew 2:1 f.

WITH THE story of the wise men, the romantic misconceptions multiply like rabbits. We are entertained by stories of the three kings, whose names are even known, namely Kaspar, Melchior, and Balthasar, and of whom one (Kaspar) is supposed to have been black, in his role as representative of the negro race. We are shown their graves in Constantinople, Milan, and Cologne. Their visit to Bethlehem has been dated on the sixth of January. And Christmas cards have been printed on which the star (with seven points!) casts its beams onto the crib like a heavenly headlight.

In Provence, France, it is thought that the three kings were descendants of the prophet Balaam, and that the gold pieces which they brought Jesus had been wrought by Terah, the father of Abraham. Joseph, the son of Jacob, is said to have given them to the people of "Sheba" when he bought spices there to embalm the body of his father. Kaspar was supposed to represent the black race, Melchior ("king of the light") the non-Semitic whites, and Balthasar (Belsazar) the Semitic peoples. Relics,

which probably were brought from Constantinople to Milan
in the fifth century, were transferred in 1164 by Rainald of
Dassel, chancellor of the Emperor Barbarossa, from Milan to
Cologne, and there regarded as evidence that Thomas the
Apostle had baptized the kings.[1]

Medieval art contributed in no small degree to the spread of
these legends. It is however not an unmixed blessing that is
afforded us here. Whenever people bury real history under the
ornament of legend, fables take the place of truth—fables which
elicit a smile from adult and reasonable people. In the twentieth
century the Church can no longer permit the miraculous elements
of Christmas to be presented in the garb of a medieval annual
fair. The Church would fail in this, for even the "simple folk"
of today are too reasonable and know too much about nature and
technology to be influenced in this way. Rather, they are inclined
to scorn these trappings, that can offer them nothing more on
Christmas Eve than would entertain a child.

Of course it would not be a pleasant task, either, to have to tell
the children, who are quite imbued with the story of the three
kings, that there were not three of them, that they weren't kings
at all, and that they didn't arrive on January sixth. This would
be such a cruel disillusionment for children that they would
perhaps infer nothing more from the new story than: It just
isn't true. Psychologically, we have then attained just the opposite
goal from what we intended: we wanted to edify, but we only
destroyed.

This problem is not easy for the Church to solve, but it is
absolutely necessary to find a solution. We cannot walk these
wrongheaded paths forever. If we make ourselves too comfortable
and, just to preserve our peace of mind, leave things as they
were even though they be false, then more and more people
will lose their faith; the thoughtful ones will easily slip through

1. Cf. H. Daniel-Rops, *Jesus and His Times*, 1944, p. 112 f.

our hands, and we will be left with the question on our conscience: Did we bring these people the whole rich truth of the "great joy," or did we obscure and bury their joy with incredible inanities? Do we bear the blame for their having gone away? Would we not heap more blame on ourselves by continuing in the same old paths? Let us proclaim the good news as it really is!

We intend to present this part of the events of Christmas in its true beauty and magnitude. What occurred will then reveal itself as far more marvelous than the charming and gay atmosphere of fable would lead us to expect. Naturally we will not turn against real miracles. The miracles reported to us by Holy Scripture, and the miracles which happen in God's realm are clear signs to us of the reality of another world. We accept them gratefully. This does not mean, however, that we have to accept uncritically every miraculous story that Christians having otherwise good intentions pass on to us. The quest for truth will be more important to us; when we investigate the "Story of the Three Wise Men" we shall find something quite different from what people have been led to believe. But what we find will be infinitely greater, more beautiful, and wonderful.

Our first task will be to clarify the dates.

The story of the magi begins with the report that Jesus was born in the days of King Herod. This king was doubtless Herod the Great, son of the Idumaean Antipater. In 47 B.C. Julius Cæsar made him procurator along with the Maccabean Hyrcanus II; he was named king by the Roman senate in 40 B.C., and died shortly before Passover in the spring of the year 4 B.C.

This fact brought about my first theological difficulty. For if Herod died *before* Christ's birth—as much as four years before— how then could he be the one responsible for the massacre of the innocents, and how could it say in Matthew that Jesus was born in the days of King Herod? Or, put more exactly, how could a king who died four years before Christ be the infanticide of

Bethlehem? It soon became evident that the answer to this question was not insuperably difficult; the solution is probably familiar to most readers.

The reckoning of time was formerly quite chaotic, and over one hundred systems for it have been noted. The best known is the Roman system, which reckons *ab urbe condita* (from the founding of the city). Terentius Varro, the presumed inventor of the Varronian system of dating, sees as the date of the founding of Rome the spring (festival of the Pallians) of the third year of the sixth Olympiad; but his "Varronian" reckoning competed with a "Capitoline" system which differed by two years. In the Greek world they counted time from the first Olympiad.

The Jews wanted to lend certainty to their time-system by beginning with the creation of the world, but were nevertheless unsure of the date of this until in the fourth century the rabbi Hillel believed he had found a fixed base. He dated Adam's creation at 3449 years "before the era of the Seleucids," which began with the fall of the year in which the Syrian Seleucus I, Nicator conquered Babylon (3449 before "Seleucus" is 3761 B.C.). The Egyptians reckoned after the Egyptian–Chaldean era of Nabonassar. It is probably not necessary to point out further the difficulties involved in all these chronological systems.

The Christian calendar stems from the abbot Dionysius Exiguus. The pope gave him the task of finding out exactly in what year Jesus was born after the founding of Rome. Dionysius gave for this the "Varronian" year of 754 *ab urbe condita*. Unfortunately, however, he erred by seven years. Christ was born 747 A.U.C. This error does not justify our calling his work bad; quite the contrary. Happily, he was mistaken by *only* seven years—it could have been by many more. Dionysius was abbot in Rome in the year 530 A.D. and died in 556. His system came only gradually into use. By the middle of the sixth century it was generally accepted in Rome; in the eighth century the

Venerable Bede was a vigorous exponent of it. The first sovereign who made occasional use of it in documents was Charlemagne. By the tenth century it was in general use throughout the western world. In Russia it was not introduced until the eighteenth century, by Peter the Great.

Dionysius made his mistake by reasoning from Luke 3:1— rightly so, in other respects—where it reads: "Now in the fifteenth year of the reign of Tiberius Cæsar" (John the Baptist began his preaching). Augustus Cæsar died on August 19 of the year 767 A.U.C. If we add fifteen years to this we get 782. According to Dionysius, Jesus began his activities in the next year, 783. Luke 3:23 says that Jesus at that time was "about thirty years of age," which Dionysius interpreted as "nearly thirty years old," namely, twenty-nine. If we subtract twenty-nine from 783 we get 754, the year which has since been the base for our calendar.

But in this calendar many mistakes lie hidden. First, Tiberius, as *collega imperii*, began his reign two years earlier than 767, namely 765. Secondly, Luke will have followed the custom in the province of Syria of dating the beginning of the year from the first of October. The fifteenth year of Tiberius is then $765+15=780$, and because of the difference in beginning the year this may have been 779. The beginning of Jesus' preaching can likewise have begun in the year 779. Moreover, Luke's expression "about thirty years of age," does not mean that he must have been *nearly* thirty years old; on the contrary, according to the rules of the land, Jesus will have been *at least* thirty years old when he entered public life, and therefore Luke's words must mean that he was over thirty years old. If we take as the year of birth 7 B.C. (747 A.U.C.), then Jesus would be, when he began to teach, thirty-two or possibly thirty-three years old.

Further difficulties lie in the fact that in early times New Year's Day, or the beginning of a new year, was very arbitrarily established, so that the length of the year and the length of the respective months were differently measured, and changes were often introduced.

The Church has known all of this for many centuries, but a change in the calendar was no longer possible in later times, and even today a correction of Dionysius' calculation, on the strength of the fact that Christ was born before the year 1, does not seem likely, even if there were real interest anywhere in this question. Besides, there is no authority which could order such a correction. Those who knew of the discrepancy may perhaps have smirked a little when in the year 1000 entire nations caught the "end of the world" mood, and gave large gifts of land and money to the church—the "end of the world" had after all occurred seven years before that time. If in the year 2000 the nations of the world get into another "end of the world panic," the "enlightened" ones will perhaps again be amused, but the mistake in the calendar will in any event not be removed.

The year of the death of Herod the Great is unmistakably fixed at 750 A.U.C. Any doubt concerning this can be ruled out, according to all historical estimates. Besides Roman accounts concerning Herod's death, we possess the detailed, and for us, important statements of Flavius Josephus. Josephus relates that Herod was ill for a rather long time before his death; at first he sought the better climate of the city of Jericho, but then, when he did not get better he visited the baths in Callirrhoe. Meeting with no improvement there he went back to Jericho, where he lay sick until the time of his death. We know that during the time of his last stay in Jericho he ordered a few insurgents burned alive, possibly followers of Judas of Galilee.

In the night after his *auto da fé* a great eclipse of the moon took place, which the people took to be a divine threat against the cruel monarch. It can be determined astronomically that of the five eclipses of the moon which were visible in Jerusalem between

8 B.C. and 2 B.C., only two come into consideration: a small one on 12-13 March, 4 B.C., and a larger one on 14-15 September, 5 B.C. The one in March has to be eliminated as coming too soon before the death of Herod: he died shortly before the Passover. From Josephus we learn that Herod's last period of illness lasted longer than this, so that the eclipse of the "divine threat" must have been that of 14-15 September in the year 5 B.C. (therefore five years before the beginning of the Dionysian calendar).

The reports concerning Herod's illness have significance for us, because from them we know that the magi did not make their visit to Herod during this illness. The visit must have occurred earlier, even earlier than Herod's *first* period of illness in Jericho. For Herod's word to the magi that he would go in person to worship the child (Mt 2:8), gives the impression that the king at that time was still quite well and could go about his official duties in Jerusalem. In this manner we arrive at the conclusion that the birth of Christ and the visit of the magi must have occurred at least six years before the beginning of our era.

The magi were by no means kings. There is not a wisp of evidence for this in ancient history. How the leap to such a conclusion could be made—and it was first made in the Middle Ages —becomes clear when we realize how Old Testament texts were arbitrarily and unhistorically applied (Ps 72:10 f.; 68:30 f.; Is 60:10 f.). Psalm 72 prophesies that the kings of Tarsis, Sheba, and Seba will bring gifts to the coming one. Isaiah names Midian, Hefa and Sheba, Kedar, Nebajoth, and Tarsis, and speaks even of gold and incense as gifts.

Matthew, who lets no opportunity slip by to show his Jewish readers which prophecies about Jesus were fulfilled, would certainly have made mention of the above prophecies, surely known to him, if in his judgment they had the slightest bearing on the story of the wise men. That he does not do so is in itself a clear indication of the incorrectness of the medieval fiction.

In any case Matthew didn't make the mistake; he and the ancients knew only too well that the countries named in the prophecies lay *in the west* and *in the south*, not *in the east*. The wise men however came from the east.

Matthew indicates that the magi in their own country had apparently pondered frequently and deeply on the "star of the king," that they definitely had Palestine in mind, and that they came to Jerusalem with the question: "Where is he that is born King of the Jews? for we have seen his star in ascension (or in the east), and are come to worship him."

How does it happen that these strangers have a close relation of this kind to the Jewish messianic prophecies and connect them with a special "royal star"?

The land of these wise men has been searched for throughout the East. To be sure, Jews lived in Arabia, Mesopotamia, Persia, etc., and they could have told of the prophecies of their fathers. But we find a satisfactory explanation only after discovering the key in the figure of the prophet Daniel. The so-called three kings were magi, i.e., priest-astrologers, Chaldeans in Babylon. We know of Daniel that among them he was a "master." To be a "master" among the magi, and from a foreign country at that, was attributable not so much to one's person, but rather more to what one knew, and what one was able to say with authority in the special province of knowledge possessed by the magi.

Daniel possessed these qualities. He knew of the prophecy of Balaam, who had foretold the Messias as the "star of Jacob"; he knew of the blessing for the whole world which would come from the king of the tribe of Juda, and he prophesied that this king would come in seventy (prophetic) weeks, i.e., in 490 years. He predicted that after the four great kingdoms the kingdom of the Messias would come. In the east these four kingdoms in Daniel were interpreted as the Persian, Median, Macedonian, and Roman realms, and it was believed that after a dreadful war against Rome the Messias would appear. That Daniel was considered a master among the priest-astrologers cannot be estimated highly enough. He exerted historically a tremendous influence. In addition it cannot be overlooked that in the large Jewish population of Mesopotamia there were even Jewish theological academies,[2] and that in these academies the Book of Daniel was considered *the* great messianic book. Daniel's prophecies dominated the pagan world of Babylonian astrology as well as the Jewish theology of the diaspora.[3]

These priest-astrologers are often called magi, but this does not mean they were sorcerers, or magicians, or the like. The caste of the Chaldeans stood in high repute in Babylon. They were the actual scholars of the realm, and their "magic" consisted in an extensive astrological evaluation of their knowledge of astronomy (by no means slight), so that their science became a religion. Therefore the word "magi" has certainly no derogatory meaning here.

The names of these wise men are not known in history. That one of the three had a black skin seems to contradict what we know of the circumstances in Babylon. There were "black" people there, but only as slaves. And one of these slaves might have been a priest? No, the medieval inventor of Kaspar pursued his Oriental studies too little; he was thinking of Saba (Seba). We owe this fiction to a European monastery; the monk who in the ninth century created Kaspar, Melchior, and Balthasar was not a wicked person, but a friendly, well-meaning man with a sense of humor. And that in addition he quickly "painted" one of his kings black had really a worthy purpose: why shouldn't the black race also be present at Christ's birth? But this "painting" took place in the Middle Ages, and ancient history tells us nothing of this.

2. Edersheim, *Life and Times*, etc., Vol. I, p. 12.
3. Cf. Pirqé de Rabbi Eliezer, c. 19, 28, 30 and 48.

The number of magi is said to have been three. But this is
also a medieval trapping. The number three was derived by
analogy with the number of gifts—gold, frankincense, and myrrh.
But that is not a valid procedure. The first centuries and subsequent tradition state no number; the only time a number is
alluded to is in talk of twelve and thirteen magi. Other accounts
mention a caravan. It is best not to try to establish a number;
it was a caravan of probably more than three priests. The kind of
bedrock certainty of finding the child that these priests had
would easily motivate several other men to join them. It was
after all a journey to find a king who was to bring salvation to
all peoples, and therefore the greatest king ever dreamed of in
Babylon.

"There is no doubt," says Theodor Zahn in his great Matthew
commentary, "that they came from some point in the kingdom
of the Parthians, who at that time ruled over all of Mesopotamia
either directly or through more or less dependent vassal princes,
such as those of Edessa and Adiabene."[4] These magi came under
the influence of the traditions of Daniel. These traditions directed
the attention of astrology to the salvation which was to come
out of the "western lands," and to "the great king who will be
born there and will bring salvation to all nations," as so many of
the inscriptions state. The magi related these royal expectations
to their astrology, which told them that the great conjunction of
Jupiter and Saturn was a star of the king; they then ascertained
that after Daniel's seventy prophetic weeks and his monarchic
prophecies the major stellar conjunction of the year 7 (B.C.) had
to mark the birth-year of the long-awaited king.

The scholars Jastrow, Jeremias, and Weidner, who have
devoted themselves to the study of Babylonian star lore, found in
the Babylonian cuneiform inscriptions numerous passages in
which the two planets are designated as "the great twins" and are

4. Th. Zahn, *Evangelium des Matthäus*, 3rd ed. 1910 p. 12.

connected with predictions of good fortune. Especially Saturn (Saturday is from "Saturn's day") was related to the West, to Syria and Palestine. Mars was considered as the "foe of Israel," Saturn as its "protector." The investigations of these and other scholars brought clearly to the fore that a close connection existed between the Babylonian star lore and the Jewish prophecies in that land, and that the meeting point of these mutual influences was always Daniel. It was he who guided the astrological expectations toward the Jewish Messias. It is very interesting to follow historically this path of astrology and its connections with the awaiting of the Messias.[5]

That the world of the Church had very little astronomical knowledge became clear not only in the Middle Ages; the venerable Church Fathers of antiquity perpetrated even greater astronomical nonsense. Ignatius relates that the star of Bethlehem surpassed all other stars and that the sun, moon, and stars "danced" about it![6] Another ancient writing had an angel appearing in the form of a star to the magi in their own country.[7] In the apocryphal book of Seth the star is described as descending, in the form of a little boy with a cross above him, onto a mountain in the Far East and summoning the magi in human language to travel to Judea.[8] Alongside this portrayal, the pointed searchlight star of medieval times could be called an improvement, although the question then arises whether Christian art is incapable of representing beauty and truth at the same time.

Understandably, much has been written about this "star." The question whether the "star" might have been a single star,

---

5. See esp. Friedr. Chr. K. H. Münter, *Stern der Weisen*, 1827; Chr. L. Ideler, *Handbuch der mathem. und technischen Chronologie*, 2 vols., 2nd ed. 1883, Vol. II, p. 399 f., and O. Gerhardt, *Der Stern des Messias*, 1922.

6. *Komm.*, *Eph.* 19 (Epistolae, 6th ed. 1920, in: *Patrum apostolicorum opera*, Vol. 2; German edition of the Letters by L. A. Winterswyl, 4th ed. 1954).

7. Evang. inf. arab., c. 7.

8. *Op. imperf.*, p. 31.

or possibly a constellation, need not concern us here. "Every good lexicon shows that the distinction between *aster* (Latin *stella*, 'single star'), and *astron* (Latin *sidus*, 'constellation') was not observed even by the best writers," declares Zahn, and he is right.[9]

Lagrange maintained that the star was a comet, e.g., Halley's Comet, which was visible there in the year 12 B.C. Apart from the fact that 12 B.C. in any case does not accord with the birth-year, and that there was no other significant comet then, it is indisputable that first, in the East a comet was regarded as an ill omen and not at all the birth star of a "king of salvation," and second, the text in Matthew unmistakably shows that the "star" was seen and could only be seen by astronomers and astrologers; the people of Jerusalem, no experts in astronomy, saw nothing in the sky, nor could they see anything. A bright comet, on the other hand, would have caught everybody's attention. For these reasons it was not a comet, nor even some kind of a "wonder star." The entire history of this makes unequivocally clear that this was an astronomical event, and one which people without astronomical knowledge could know nothing about.

An astronomical event, which explains the references in Matthew and helps fix the birth year of Jesus, actually did occur in history, namely the major conjunction of Jupiter and Saturn in the year 747 A.U.C., therefore in the year 7 before our era. Oswald Gerhardt explains in his fine book "that Saturn alone forms the central point of the whole, for only its conjunction with Jupiter in the sign of Pisces had been related to the birth of the Messias, and that in no other year than 7 B.C. did any astronomical, or astrologically meaningful phenomenon occur except the already known Saturn-Jupiter conjunction."[10] We find this astronomical explanation confirmed in every respect.

9. Th. Zahn, *Evangelium des Lukas*, 1913, p. 93.
10. O. Gerhardt, *Der Stern des Messias*, p. 67.

The "major" conjunctions occurring in three phases are rare (no special astrological meaning is ascribed to the "minor" conjunctions); therefore they could also be considered as "stars of the king." The next major conjunction will take place in 1981, and following that, in 2238. Astronomy, to the extent it does not become immersed in speculation, is the most exact of all sciences; it is pure mathematics, and its calculations can be relied upon. It tells us concerning the major conjunction of 7 B.C. that the double star in the Near East was continuously visible on any clear night for nine months from the beginning of April, and could be observed sometimes before and sometimes after midnight, and at times throughout the entire night.

The magi said: "We have seen his star in the ascension" (Mt 2:2). The Greek has *en te anatole*, which can be translated by "in the East," but actually the magi expressed themselves more astronomically. By *anatole* (the ascending) the beginning of the conjunction is meant, namely the stage at which the stars began to approach each other. The three phases of the major conjunction could be precisely followed in their "rising" and "setting." The end of May and the beginning of June marked the first phase, the twenty-sixth of September to about October sixth marked the second, and the third lasted approximately from December fifth until a few days after the fifteenth of December.

Actually these termini should be fixed even further back in time, for Bouché-Leclercq demonstrates from Ptolemy and other sources[11] that, according to the astrologers of that time, a conjunction began as soon as the two stars had approached one another to three degrees; that would put the beginning of the first phase of the conjunction back to April 25, 7 B.C.; and the moment which the magi mean when they say : We have seen his star "in the ascent" (*en te anatole*), is even somewhat earlier.

11. A. Bouché Leclercq, *L'astrologie grecque*, 1899 (on Mt 2, 1–12).

Gerhardt confirms this: "In strict observance of their laws our magi had to fix that moment when the messias-planet (Saturn), shortly before entry into the conjunction itself, was again visibly ascending within the sign of Pisces for the first time" [*on April* 23].[12]

That is why the magi saw the star of the king on the twenty-third of April in its *anatole*. They resolved to attend to it, and came with their questions to Jerusalem.

> But when King Herod heard this, he was troubled, and so was all Jerusalem with him.
>
> Matthew 2:3

Herod was then sixty-six years of age and was surnamed "the Great." History has left him this name, possibly only to be able to distinguish him better from the many rulers of the same name. Although he was anything but a noble figure, he occupied a special place in the history of the Jewish realm. He came as a Roman agent to Israel; he was the son of the Idumaean Antipater and therefore, as the Jews also called him, an Edomite; he was made procurator in 47 B.C. along with the feeble-minded Maccabean prince Hyrcanus II. At that time he was twenty-six (born 73 B.C.). At the same time he was governor of Galilee, and also received Samaria and Coele-Syria under his control, so that his realm in its external borders was like King David's realm.

His opponents were weak. The famous Hasmonaean House of the Maccabees ("hammer of war"), which for some time played a role in Israel similar to the one played in the Netherlands by the House of Orange, and whose heroes had given their possessions and lives in many a fight for freedom, had by now nearly died out, and those that were still left in that heroic tribe

12. O. Gerhardt, *op. cit.*, p. 69.

did not have the importance of their ancestors. The successor of the weak Hyrcanus II was his granddaughter, the princess Mariamne, and thus heiress of the ancient splendor.

Herod, although despised as an Idumaean and agent of Rome, knew how to conquer this heiress, whom he passionately loved in his own way. The poor princess apparently was not able to refuse this marriage under the prevailing circumstances. Thus Herod became prince consort, but that was not enough for him. In the year 40 he was named king by the Senate in Rome and was now "of equal rank" with Mariamne. To be sure, this was not true in the eyes of his subjects. Whenever he and Queen Mariamne appeared among the people, the applause and cheers were for her—Herod was scarcely noticed.

He took his revenge. He had almost all the members of the Hasmonaean house murdered: his wife Mariamne, also the old prince Hyrcanus II, his brother-in-law Aristobulus and the latter's mother, Alexandra. And when the people transferred their love for Mariamne to her sons Alexander and Aristobulus, Herod had these assassinated also. Vengeful and filled with a blood lust, he was ruthless to the point of murder.

Well known are the ironic words of the Emperor Augustus, who knew quite well what went on in Herod's realm: "I would rather be one of Herod's pigs than his son."[13] Pork was carefully avoided by this half-Jew, who liked to play the Jew, as being lawfully unclean; but Herod's sons did not enjoy even this protection. Herod needed no court of justice. The assassins of his victims acted on his command, and if he wanted to make sure no one learned, for example, just how the drowning of a Hasmonaean while at his bath had occurred, he did not refrain from having the assassins murdered by still other assassins, so that there would be no witnesses.

He got along fairly well with the priestly class in Jerusalem,

13. *Melius est Herodis porcum esse quam filium;* in Macrobius, *Sat.* II, 4, 11.

for they supported his machinations. The successful agent of Rome was good enough for these priests to marry their princess Mariamne. And Herod purchased their support to a considerable extent by the erection of buildings, especially the magnificent temple which he ordered to be built for Jerusalem and the priests.

Biblically speaking, it was actually not allowable to tear down the old temple of Zorobabel, for the prophecy was that in *this* temple the Messias would appear. The king and the priests nevertheless found a way to remain "biblical" and yet build a new temple. With the approval of the priests Herod had each stone of the Zorobabel temple "exchanged" for a new one, stone by stone, so that the temple was never really "absent," and yet disappeared completely. In this way they thought to avoid the religious difficulty. The priests "justified" the building with appropriate texts and were exceedingly pleased over the beautiful, representative, and immense structure that became the pride of the city. They rewarded the vain and ambitious Herod with the title "the Great," in itself the least costly imaginable compensation, yet one eagerly accepted by this king. One gets the impression that the king and the priests of Jerusalem deserved each other. The people were probably not in accord with all of this, but king and priests after all had the power, and knew how to make use of it for themselves.

Although they knew him well, the Romans made use of this ruthless ruler for their own purposes for many years. It is easy to see why. The Jews were a very refractory people, and it was a diplomatic problem of the first order to maintain peace and order among them. The Romans saw in Herod a very useful tool for this task. The Jews hated him much too much to regard him as their champion of freedom; on the other hand, he knew the customs of the Jews well enough to come to terms with them more easily than the Romans could. Besides, through the marriage to Mariamne he was the legal ruler. And finally, the

Romans knew he was able to get along with the Jewish priests. With his help, peace and calm were fairly successfully preserved in the land.

Now suddenly the wise men from the East came on the scene and asked about him who was to be king of the Jews. Herod was alarmed, and with him all Jerusalem!

We can understand Herod's alarm. A new-born king of the Jews would have to be his enemy. Add to this the fact that he first heard the news from foreigners—he had known nothing about this until then—and we can see this must have made him even angrier and more suspicious. That all Jerusalem was alarmed along with him could mean in itself that the populace feared this news could release fresh killings and bloodshed throughout the land; possibly there actually were Jerusalemites who were afraid for this reason. But to interpret the text this way is to do that city too much honor. A group of priests lived there who, because of the beautiful new temple and its lucrative revenues, gladly compromised with Herod, and even after Mariamne's murder found excuses to soothe their consciences with. These corrupt priests were afraid for the same reasons that Herod was.

> And gathering together all the chief priests and Scribes of the people, he [Herod] inquired of them where the Christ was to be born.[14]
>
> Matthew 2:4

The old king learned quickly enough whom this news concerned. In his conversation with the wise men he probably learned more than the short account given in Matthew. They doubtless told him of the ancient prophecies and of their own

14. It is worth noting that the passage from Micah 5 differs in some respects from the Hebrew text as well as from the LXX; Matthew apparently quotes very freely, but probably took his text from the targum.

expectations. The king understood exactly what they were seeking, and he knew the Jews and their writings well enough to know that the Messias was meant. Such talk was not new to him for every revolutionary proclaimed himself a messias, and Herod knew how to cope with such situations. Indeed, this time it could be the real Messias, as the simple wise men from the East seemed to think; but that did not disturb him.

"Where will the Messias be born?" Herod asks the scribes and the high priests. It is a brutal question, actually an insult to the priests and scribes, for with it the old assassin seems to say: Of course, we will set about together to kill this Messias. With that question he takes for granted their betrayal of the belief in a Messias. And—he knows his people. Although the lords of the Sanhedrin knew very well what Herod intended doing and would do, they nonetheless provided him, Bible in hand, with their expert theological explanation. They said to him:

> "In Bethlehem of Judea; for thus it is written through the prophet, 'And thou, Bethlehem, of the land of Juda, art by no means least among the princes of Juda; For from thee shall come forth a leader who shall rule my people Israel.'"
>
> Matthew 2:5 f.; cf. Micah 5:2

These were the guardians of the divine word, the religious leaders of the people of the ancient covenant! This was the sacred synod of Israel! These priests could not beg to be excused; they knew what was at stake. The brutal question of the king left their sacred views unscathed, and more than this, they made common cause with him. Herod didn't know the exact location of the Messias' birthplace; he had of course heard about it and also knew that these things played a role in rabbinical theology. His Jewish cohorts however could give him more complete information, given their knowledge, and this they did without restraint.

They knew he would instigate murder, but this did not disturb them. If Herod wanted to murder, let him do it. They were not guilty of it, for after all, they had only said where the Messias would be born. Anyway, so they consoled themselves, the real Messias would know how to take care of himself. Naturally, outward appearances were preserved: the Bible lay on the table, the king did not say that he would kill the child, officially therefore the synod knew nothing of this, and could begin with prayer and end with praise and thanksgiving.

What monstrous hypocrisy! It was not the first, nor would it be the last time in history that religious leaders and dignitaries gave themselves over to more evil things than the worst worldlings had ever done. When Jesus later (Mt 23) delivers his scathing reprimand against these people, he calls them: "Ye serpents, ye generation of vipers"; many times the sermon contains the word "hypocrites," and we need hardly be surprised if the synod just described was vividly recalled to mind.

The scribes were entrusted with the interpretation of Micah 5:2. We get an even stronger impression of the mentality of these spiritual leaders when we take the trouble to examine rabbinical literature to see whether their grasp of the Messianic prophecies was merely cursory, or very thorough. It was in fact quite thorough. We possess a collection of their explanations of Messianic texts in the well-known rabbinical document *Yalkut Shimeoni*.[15] We read how the rabbis found 456 Messianic prophecies in the Old Testament: 75 in the Pentateuch, 243 in the prophets, and 138 in the rest of the Old Testament writings. In addition they derived 558 Messianic allusions from Old Testament texts. That this exegetical literature fills an entire library proves with what diligence the scribes devoted themselves to the interpretation of the prophecies.

15. Published in Frankfurt in 1787; treated in detail in Edersheim, II, p. 710 f.

Naturally the explanation of Micah 5:2 occupies a prominent place in the literature (recapitulated in the *Targum Pirqé* of Rabbi Eliezer, *c.* 3, and in many other places). The members of the synod actually didn't have to search long for an answer to Herod's question, for it concerned one of the main topics of their lifelong research. They were actually so proud of the fruits of their work that they dared to write that God himself, out of respect for the intellectual prowess of the chosen people, devoted several hours each day to the study of the law according to Jewish interpretation (Targum ps. Jon. for Dt 32:4, Abhodah Zarath, etc.); indeed, they claimed that God studied the Old Testament by day, and by night the six rabbinical treatises of the Mishna (Targum for Hl 5, 10), only to learn how he might correctly fulfill the prophecies. . . .

The oddest thing about these sedulous scholars is that they give the impression of being thoroughly convinced of the truth of their arrogant opinions! They demonstrate how ruinous to religion too great an emphasis on intellect can become. These men had such an exalted opinion of their intellectual accomplishments that they really believed God couldn't get along without them. How little they knew of what God is really like is shown in the course of their synod under Herod. Of course, there may have been men present at this synod who temporarily bowed to the majority, and didn't have the courage to resist, but who later gave conscientious witness to the truth. Perhaps among them were Joseph of Arimathea and Gamaliel.

> Then Herod summoned the Magi secretly, and carefully ascertained from them the time when the star had appeared to them. And sending them to Bethlehem, he said, "Go and make careful inquiry concerning the child, and when you have found him, bring me word, that I too may go and worship him." Now they, having heard the king, went their way.
>
> Matthew 2:7–9

Herod wanted more exact information. He did this secretly, i.e., not in a large assembly, but in a private audience which gave him the opportunity to win the confidence of the strangers and induce them to talk.

The wise men will have doubtless answered him heavy of heart, for although they were not very familiar with the circumstances in Jerusalem, they surely sensed that their high hopes and joyous expectations were not fully shared. They no doubt were amazed that the fulfillment of the promise that caused them to journey so far was apparently new and hitherto unknown in Israel itself, even among the priests. It would have been quite understandable to the magi if Jerusalem had received them with joy and festivities. The king of the Jews was born, and the Jews were the first among God's peoples! But see: the Jews knew nothing about it, although they knew the whole Bible and all the prophets and therefore should have known more than the foreign astrologers with their scanty information. And when the Jews now heard of the fulfillment, their alarm at the news must have struck the wise men as odd. The latter must have thought, how is this possible? Have we allowed our heads to be turned by empty and barren illusions there in distant Babylon? What shall we make of all this?

Herod made detailed inquiry of these men. He may have heard with a smile the talk of the strange stellar conjunction and the interpretation by the wise men of the star of the king. Astrology was of course not unknown to the Romans, but cultivated people regarded it as a game, the childish nonsense of a barbaric culture, that needn't be taken seriously. Nevertheless, Herod wanted exact information regarding their calculations and their plans. His suspicious nature and his royal interests compelled him to curiosity, and so he listened to everything. Finally he dismissed the strangers with the nice, polite promise that he himself would go to pay homage to the child. Whether he was able to say that with solemn mien, we do not know. The wise men at any rate seemed to take him at his word.

We can scarcely assume that Herod would immediately take to the sword. The whole story would be to him, the cultivated Roman, worth no more than an amused smile. And even if the real Messias of Israel had been born, then he still had time. He knew now about how old the baby would be; born at the appearance of the star, it couldn't have been more than a few months old, and so it would be quite a while yet before this alleged Messias would seize the sword and become dangerous. He now had information, and at the proper time would know how to root out the danger before it became imminent. Meanwhile he had other and more important things to do.

We must admire the magi for continuing their journey to Bethlehem, and not turning back disillusioned to their country after all they had experienced, or at least suspected. Luckily, Herod did not send an observer along with them to Bethlehem. He could have done so; Bethlehem was a mere two hours' journey away on foot. And if the matter had seemed somewhat more important to him at the time, he no doubt would have taken this precaution. Apparently the king only believed history half-way, and in any case did not ascribe much significance to it.

> Now they [the wise men], having heard the king, went their way. And behold, the star that they had seen in the East went before them, until it came and stood over the place where the child was. And when they saw the star they rejoiced exceedingly.
>
> Matthew 2:9–10

The wise men hastily departed Herod's city. A small but important note lies in the report that they saw the "star." Then it must have been dark. People in sub-tropical lands do in fact journey oftener in the evening because of the day's heat (here again an indication that Jesus was born in the summer). But there was likely another factor involved, too. We get the impression that the magi, after their conversation with the king, could no longer endure their stay in the city—and that speaks well for them. Herod was courteous, but sincere men can easily sense polite hypocrisy. Besides, in the meantime they could have learned more about the situation in Herod's realm.

It is easy to imagine that these strangers, who were seeking great and holy things, could no longer remain in the atmosphere of Jerusalem. Perhaps they were also afraid that something might intervene—the king might either forbid their journey at the last moment, or provide an accompanying guard of soldiers. After all their disillusionment in the capital city, they could easily have been assailed by doubts and fears. We meet them again, in any case, in the evening on the road to Bethlehem, perhaps in the evening of the same day they spoke with the king.

That they left in the evening in order to see the star is an unwarranted assumption. As Matthew strikingly reports, the sight of the star afforded them very great joy, therefore also a very great surprise, which they were not expecting at that moment. Everything that they had encountered up to now must have made them uncertain as to whether it was worth it to continue the journey. After all, Bethlehem had been mentioned to them by people who in no way shared their beliefs and their hopes, and who did not think of joining them on their way to Bethlehem, perhaps merely scoffed at their journey. They might have been even deliberately misled as to their destination. Nevertheless, they set out on their way, and behold: the star, the star of the king appeared anew.

Apparently these magi were not yet in a position to calculate in advance precisely the days and hours of the conjunction, as astronomers are capable of doing today. They did know that the "great" conjunction would repeat itself three times in the same year. They saw in the east the *anatole*, the ascension, the first stage. Without doubt they were therefore awaiting the second stage. But it was a great surprise to them, one that made them "rejoice with exceeding great joy," when this second stage occurred just as they were journeying from Jerusalem to Bethlehem. The element of surprise lay not in the conjunction itself, but in its occurrence at that particular moment.

Coincidence or miracle? This problem surely did not exist for the magi. And anyone who reflects deeply on this event will find the answer in the facts themselves. The event is a miraculous event, in which nature with her laws serves a far-seeing Providence.

The exceeding great joy of the magi springs from their gratitude for this wonder, which promised rich fulfillment to their hopes: You have seen the star of the King in its ascension, and now you see it once more: The King is really here.

It is, of course, in non-astrological and non-astronomical terms that we are told how the star preceded the wise men and led them to their destination. Matthew relates the true story just as he had heard it from Mary and Joseph, simply and beautifully. The astronomical aspect of the event is up to us to work out, and this is possible without great difficulty.

We have already established earlier that the wise men resolved on the twenty-third of April to set out on their original journey. Assuming that preparations for the caravan might have taken a certain amount of time, say, a few months, and adding to this an estimated six to eight weeks for the actual trip, then we arrive at a time within the period of the second stage of the conjunction (from September twenty-sixth to about October sixth). Oswald Gerhardt describes the relevant conditions of time and place as follows:

"The distance between Jerusalem and Bethlehem is five miles, which a person on foot could traverse in barely two hours, a caravan camel in one and two-third hours. In this one and two-third hours the pair of planets describes 3/10 of its path across the sky. Just before reaching Bethlehem the road makes a gradual winding ascent to the town. The two hills, on which the town is situated, lie respectively 2,542 and 2,715 feet above sea level, and thus 106 to 295 feet above the level of the road. The road runs on an average from north to south. In their one and two-third hour trip the magi could follow that 3/10 of the planetary path until they reached Bethlehem, when the two planets were at their meridian. . . .

"When the magi set out that evening on their expectant journey, they observed how the constellation gradually approached the point above the hills where Bethlehem lies, during the same time they themselves hastened to that same place . . . The question arises: How high was the constellation in the sky then? Was it not perhaps obscured for our travelers by the hills of Bethlehem? The highway has an ascending grade of 20 to 30%. The star was at a point, for example on September six, located at 52.2 degrees above the horizon, and maintained that height throughout the months of September, October, and November . . . Both hills would not have blocked the constellation from the view of the wise men . . . In any case, no matter which hill was involved, they saw their star, when it was at its meridian, above one part of the city, and in just that part lay the house of the Holy Family.

"The months of July and August," Gerhardt goes on to say, "are excluded from consideration in my opinion, because then our magi would not have left Jerusalem until or after midnight, which is unlikely. The time from December fifteen on is also eliminated, because in January definitely, and in December very probably, the constellation would not have been visible until after it had already passed the meridian . . . If we knew exactly at what hour and minute the magi observed the 'standing still' [meridian] of the constellation, then it would be possible for us to determine the exact day. As it is, we can only say that the end of September best fits the facts and is the most probable time."[16]

Perhaps it would be possible to ascertain the day more closely, but the planetary tables[17] show us that conjunctions are seen differently from every point of the earth and therefore cannot be fixed with absolute certainty; moreover, it would not help much to know whether the wise men were in Bethlehem on the twenty-sixth, twenty-seventh or twenty-eighth of September, especially since the exact date of Jesus' birth couldn't be derived with certainty from the date of their visit, anyway. We therefore will content ourselves with the fact that the visit of the magi took place at the end of September.

How the wise men found the dwelling they were looking for is easy to explain without astronomical information. In that small village, where everyone knew of the stories of the shepherds, and the wonders surrounding the birth were on the lips of all, a single question would be enough to bring forth the answer: Of course we can tell you that—right there in the grotto of that caravansary, in a manger; you will find the baby there. Just go there and celebrate with us; the child is from the royal line of our great king David!

The wise men no doubt sensed a spirit here in Bethlehem different from the one in Jerusalem. The first person they happened to question was no doubt happy to tell them what the whole village knew. Anyway that kind of a caravan would not arrive unnoticed in a village like Bethlehem; naturally word got around quickly. Bethlehem heard of a caravan coming from the East which would pay homage to the child born on that miraculous night seen by the shepherds. The news of the caravan,

---

16. Gerhardt, p. 67 f.

17. *Planetentafeln für jedermann zur Berechnung der geozentrischen Orte der grozen Planeten und des Mondes für den Zeitraum von* 3400 *v. Chr. bis* 2600 *n. Chr.*, drawn up by Karl Schoch, 1927.

combined with the news of other previous happenings, must have afforded the shepherds and inhabitants of Juda new things to think upon. The words, "the promised Messias," had become an open secret.

It is unlikely that the magi made their visit that same evening. It is possible in itself, but it would have gone against the customs of the time. Somewhat further on in the text of Matthew we read that the magi received the warning "in a dream" to take a different route for their return journey, so they must have slept a night after their visit. We can visualize it best as having happened this way: the magi arrived in the evening in Bethlehem, stayed there overnight, and after good oriental custom made their visit of homage to the child, and then in the following night had the dream containing the warning.

It is worthy of note that Matthew, who step by step shows the fulfillment of the prophecies in the life of Jesus, might also here have found opportunity to say: Then was fulfilled what was said by the prophet: "A star will arise out of Jacob's line." But he refrains from this here. Apparently he did not intend imprinting a divine seal on astrological star lore; he simply accepted the fact as it was.

> And entering the house, they [the wise men] found the child with Mary his mother, and falling down they worshipped him. And opening their treasures they offered him gifts of gold, frankincense and myrrh.
>
> Matthew 2:11

Matthew speaks of a "house," and many have inferred from this that Joseph and Mary had moved from the stable or grotto into a house. That is possible. The registration may have been earlier, and people who had already registered would gradually have left the village. But for Matthew the word "house" was a general term that could also mean the lodging in the grotto.

Joseph and his family did indeed "reside" there. Moreover we have already seen that living there need not have been so primitive as we might imagine. Finally, living conditions in the sub-tropical east in the first century were such that there was not much difference between living in a grotto and in a "dwelling."

Although the Bethlehemites, even the shepherds, were not Bedouins,[18] it would be mistaken to imagine their life as being luxurious. For one thing, they were not rich enough, and for another, luxury in those difficult times was even dangerous. We may infer from the tenor of the gospel account that Joseph and Mary did not move immediately from the sacred birthplace of the promised one to someplace else. Here, where God gave them the son of the promise, they would gladly stay as long as they remained in Bethlehem. Joseph, incidentally, is not mentioned in this account, but that does not mean he wasn't there; Matthew mentions only the chief personages, Mary and the child.

Naturally there would have been much discussion during the wise men's visit. They had a right to learn what Joseph and Mary knew, and Joseph and Mary for their part would want to know what led the magi to them from a distant land. The angelic visitations, the wonders on the night of Jesus' birth— all these things the wise men would carry back with them to their country. Joseph and Mary heard new things that they would ponder and keep in their hearts. And the wise men worshipped the child: they knew and believed. They had found what they hoped to find.

The magi brought wonderful gifts: gold, frankincense, and myrrh. Of course gold was a useful gift; it must have been helpful to Joseph during the flight to Egypt. But why did they bring frankincense and myrrh? Both were regarded in the Orient as precious gifts (cf. Is 60:6; Ps 72:15; Jer 6:20; Hb 3:6; Sir 24:15). Did the wise men want to express a deeper meaning by

18. Cf. G. Dalman, *Orte und Wege Jesu*, 3rd ed. 1924, p. 44 f.

these gifts? The unusual significance attributed in those times to gifts of incense and myrrh has repeatedly given rise to the supposition that a special symbolic character attached to both those gifts of the wise men. Incense and myrrh were valued at secular and religious feasts because of their fragrance; also, myrrh was used in the anointing of the dead (Jn 19:39) and mixed as a narcotic with the wine at the crucifixion (Mk 15:23).

The Church Fathers concluded from this that with the gold the wise men honored Jesus as king, with the incense as God, and with the myrrh as savior; and they combined with this the view that we thereby should offer Jesus the gold of our love, the incense of our prayers, and the myrrh of our mortification. With all its beauty, this interpretation still leaves the question unanswered as to why the wise men chose these gifts, and whether we can really ascribe such symbolism to their motives as the Church Fathers did.

On the other hand it is certain that these magi regarded the kingdom of the new-born king as more spiritual than "ordinary" strangers ever would have done. Their gifts of incense and myrrh indicate that they did not conceive this kingdom as an earthly kingdom, but understood it rather in a priestly sense. What the disciples of Jesus learned only gradually and laboriously seems to have been grasped already in principle by these wise men in Babylon. Their gifts foreshadow symbolically a special kingdom of a spiritual kind. Perhaps the wise men were only dimly conscious of this, and they intuitively chose gifts which were not entirely of a worldly character. That they did so at least expresses their inner attitude, and also Joseph and Mary were probably aware of this.

And being warned in a dream not to return to Herod, they went back to their own country by another way.

Matthew 2:12

In avoiding Jerusalem, the magi probably made the return journey via Jericho. After that the wise men disappear from the story as we know it. Unfortunately, the Acts of the Apostles tells us only a fraction of the apostolic work. To be sure, Luke tells us much about Paul, and even some of Peter's activities, but of the rest of the apostles we hear next to nothing. If we also possessed an "Acts of the Apostles" about the work of Saint Thomas, the apostle of the East, and about Thaddaeus, known in some manuscripts as Lebbaeus ("the courageous one") and mentioned in Luke 6:16 as Judas of James (Judas, the son of a certain James), for which reason the name Judas Thaddaeus is mostly used of this apostle active in Mesopotamia, then we would probably know further details about the wise men. Some news did reach us, nonetheless.

In Mesopotamia, the country of the wise men, Thaddaeus must have found favorable conditions for the reception of his evangel, for large and thriving Christian churches quickly appeared there. In the year 50 A.D. a Babylonian prince, Izates of Adiabene was converted to Judaism, convinced by what was reported to him of the new-born king of the Jews. In 66 A.D. the priest king Tiridates (this time a magi who was also a king!) traveled from the land of the Parthians (Armenia) to Rome, to pay homage to "king" Nero. This journey was expressly motivated by his reading in the stars of the expected world king in the west. When he then learns from the wise men and the apostles in the east that their king had been crucified, he wished quickly to make reparation for the "error" of the wise men, traveled to Rome and paid homage to—Nero! Of course Nero was uncommonly flattered to be greeted by the wise king from the east as the king of salvation born in the west.

What tradition tells of Abgar Ukkama is also interesting. King Abgar Ukkama ("the black one") ruled from 13 to 50 A.D. in Edessa, in northern Mesopotamia. We wonder, by the way, whether the Middle Ages in inventing the black magi Kaspar perhaps knew something of the black Abgar; even the names have a certain similarity. At any rate, this Abgar was not a negro, but was called black because of his black hair. This Abgar is said to have corresponded with Jesus, and to have asked Jesus in his letter to cure him of his illness, and in exchange for this to have offered his kingdom as a place of refuge. Jesus is supposed to have answered that because of his mission he was obliged to stay in Jerusalem, but that after his ascension he would send one of his disciples to heal the king; Jesus is also said to have sent him a picture of himself.

This correspondence was taken quite seriously in those early centuries. Eusebius, the great historian, considered it genuine and published it from the archives of Edessa. The eastern churches even today have their "Abgarus pictures" of the Lord. Today we know that both correspondence and picture are not genuine. But there is certainly an element of truth in the story: first, the fact that Abgar XV was a Christian; second, that Judas Thaddaeus was able to establish a thriving Christian church in Abgar's kingdom; and third, if we view all of this against the background of what is reported in Matthew 2:1–21, we are not in the realm of mere conjecture to say that apparently the visit of the magi in Bethlehem had a very widespread and lasting effect.

In what does the greatness and significance of the magi consist? After the gospel first tells how Jesus came to us, these men show us how we are to come to Jesus. Suppose we picture to ourselves the following sharp contrasts: On the one hand we have the Jews in Jerusalem with the Old Testament as a precious possession, prepared for centuries for the arrival of Jesus, God's chosen people, and—they know nothing of the birth, in the presence of Herod have to consult the prophetic writings, where they find the pertinent passages readily enough, but nevertheless misuse them. They do not think of going to Bethlehem. On the other hand we have astrologers from a foreign country, who know only a little of Israel's prophecies, but enough to travel from Babylon to Israel, and who despite all disappointments come to Bethlehem and actually find and worship the king in the manger. From this we can see that the Christian religion is neither Christian nor a religion if it is not in our hearts and does not impel our hearts to a genuine search for God.

In the Jewish shepherds and in the wise men from the East we find Jewish Christians and Gentile Christians, so to speak, united from the very beginning at the crib of Jesus. However much they may have struggled later to preserve this unity, it was here already established and sanctified by God. It is not so much a tribute to the accuracy of their astrology that these wise men actually reached Bethlehem; rather, we realize here the truth of Jesus' words: "Ask, and it shall be given you; seek, and ye shall find; knock, and it shall be opened unto you" (Mt 7:7).

Astrology is superstition. These priests possessed only a seed of truth in a granary full of superstitions, but their sincerely searching spirits caused that seed to grow; they sought, and they found. A whole host of heathenry in the head cannot destroy a grain of truth when the heart and soul seek God. Conversely, Jerusalem showed that a head full of truth, without a heart really desiring God, cannot reach Bethlehem and must even sit by and watch while the "last" of Babylon become the "first" before the children of Israel.

We spoke of miraculous happenings, and said that greater miracles occurred here than could ever be painted in pictures. The entire course of events revealed a marvelous harmony that makes us ask: was this coincidence or miracle?

Anyone mindful of Jesus' words: "Seek, and ye shall find," will discern here the divine Providence, who sees to it that people who really seek will really find. Here "coincidence" reveals itself as "miracle." This is not to say that in the creation of the world,

God so arranged the day of that major conjunction that it would coincide with the journey of the magi from Jerusalem to Bethlehem. His main purpose in creation and the history of the world is that men who really seek, really find. For the great God nothing is too small and nothing too great; the smallest as well as the greatest can serve his loving purposes. That becomes historically apparent here: It belongs to "that which was from the beginning, which we have heard, which we have seen with our eyes, which we have looked upon, and our hands have handled, of the Word of Life" (1 Jn 1:1).

It is worthy of note how the relationship, noted above, between the Danielian prophecies and Babylonian astrology has strongly influenced later Jewish history.

Thus we read for example in Rabbi Abraham ben Chijja of Spain (d. ca. 1136) that he expected the arrival of the Messias in 1464 A.D. during the major conjunction of Saturn and Jupiter of that year. Moses ben Maimon, his famous contemporary, alludes to him and says "that this kind of expectation recurs among Jews of all lands." Many Jewish scholars have written in the same vein, and their thoughts continually center about Daniel's prophecies and the great conjunction of Saturn and Jupiter we are familiar with.

Very striking are the meditations of the well-known Jewish commentator Abarbanel (or Abrabanel), born 1437, died 1508, who, by the way, entertained no sympathies for Christianity. In his commentary on Daniel he points out that the major conjunction of Jupiter and Saturn in the sign of Pisces in 747 A.U.C. had particular reference to Israel. He adduces five mystical reasons for this. He further says that the conjunctions of these two planets can be called small, medium, great, very great, and mighty. The latter occur at intervals of 2860 years; then, after the completion of twelve great conjunctions a meeting of the two planets would follow as a mighty sign of the beginning of the entire cycle. Abarbanel calculated that the previous "mighty" conjunction took place in the Jewish year 2365 (1396 B.C.), "when Israel was in Egypt, three years before the birth of our lord Moses," and therefore expected the next one in the year 5224 (1464 A.D.). "There is no doubt," he says, "that the time is at hand for the birth of the man of God, the Messias, who is our justice, greater than Abraham and more exalted than Moses."

Abarbanel recited in great detail how in the old Midrashim[19] the so-called Messias-Haggadah occurs, in which the birth of the Messias is connected with a star appearing in the East. Thus we see how closely Daniel's prophecies and Babylonian star-lore were interwoven and how later history confirms and throws light on our exposition.

On the Christian side we have the writings of Petrus Alliaco (Pierre d'Ailly), Pico della Mirandola, and Riccioli concerning the star of the Messias. But these ideas found universal interest when the great astronomer Johann Kepler in 1606 declared in his work *De Stella Nova* (Prague) that the above noted major conjunction was the star of the wise men. Since then the discovery was regarded as "official" for the scientific world. As we have seen, it has indeed proved valid and contributed in great degree to an historically exact understanding of the events of Christmas.

"Let us summarize briefly the entire occurrence," says Gerhardt: "In the year 7 before our era there took place a conjunction of Saturn and Jupiter in Pisces, which in every respect accords with the partly astrological, partly astronomical passages in Matthew. The star which referred to the Messias-king was Saturn; that phenomenon referred to his birth was the conjunction; the decisive moment was the appearance of Saturn in the *anatole* ; astronomical calculations confirm it all exactly,

19. *Bethha-Midrasch*, ed. by Jellinek, 1853-1878.

point for point. Likewise the statements in Matthew concerning
the movement and position of the constellation on the southern
horizon of Jerusalem are in accord with those calculations. Thus
it is historically and mathematically shown that in the gospel
there is a fact from which it can be inferred that Jesus was born
in the year 7 before our era. This conclusion is further
strengthened by the fact that later generations had certain
knowledge of this astronomical phenomenon, and by the fact
that this same year can be ascertained also in other ways as the
year of Jesus' birth."[20]

20, Gerhardt, p. 88 f.

CHAPTER V

IN THE TEMPLE

And when the days of her purification were fulfilled according
to the Law of Moses, they took him up to Jerusalem to present
him to the Lord—as it is written in the Law of the Lord, "Every
male that opens the womb shall be called holy to the Lord"—
and to offer a sacrifice according to what is said in the Law of the
Lord, "a pair of turtle-doves or two young pigeons."

Luke 2:22–24

IN LUKE the coming of the magi is not mentioned, while
Matthew does not mention the trip to the temple on the fortieth
day. Neither evangelist bothers to explain the differences in the
two accounts, and it is just as well, for this shows each wrote
independently of the other. The occasional congruences and
differences permit the authenticity and truth to stand out more
sharply. In any event, the trip to the temple belongs to the
historical events surrounding the event of Christmas and fits in
well with the whole.

It is clear from the entire pattern of events that the visit of
the wise men took place *before* the temple visit. If the visit of
the wise men is fixed at the end of September, then the visit
to the temple probably took place in the first week of October
(and therefore the birth of Jesus at the end of August).

Bound by tradition and faithful to the law, Joseph remained

in Bethlehem until he and Mary could go with the child to the temple on the fortieth day.

That Joseph intended staying in Bethlehem even after that, does not accord with the sense of the story, nor would it have been actually advisable. Joseph knew that he dared not stay longer in Judea and in the vicinity of Jerusalem. He knew well enough the dangerous Herod. Even as a descendant of David he was not safe, and now the events of Christmas night created even more danger. He was aware of the talk going on about these things; the homage paid by the wise men would alone be sufficient, he presumed, to cause a stir in Judea and Jerusalem. In Galilee he would be definitely freer and safer.

What happened in the meantime to his carpenter's trade in Nazareth is not known; most likely one or more of his sons by his first marriage was "minding the store," so that the workshop would not be abandoned even in the absence of their father. But everything drew him back to Nazareth, where he was used to living and working. We may assume that he waited the forty days in Bethlehem, heavy of heart and yet resolved to observe the law, and after that intended to return to Nazareth. It was his fidelity to the law that kept Joseph in Bethlehem.

This motive fits very well the image that we have been able to form of Joseph, and demonstrates anew that he deserved his epithet "the righteous," just like his son James, primarily because of his exemplary faithfulness to the law. To be sure, he was taking a risk going to the temple, and he knew exactly what was at stake; but for the fulfillment of this sacred duty to accompany mother and child to the temple, he counted strongly on God's help.

According to Leviticus 12:1-3, a woman who had brought a child into the world was impure for seven days, and therefore was obliged to remain away from the sanctuary for thirty-three days thereafter. At the time of her purification (purification actually meant: Release from the obligations of the law), she was to sacrifice a yearling lamb and a dove, and if she was poor, two doves. The presentation of the man child to the Lord is stipulated in Exodus 13:12. Luke combines both requirements into one. While in the book of Leviticus the emphasis is on the purification of the mother, Luke stresses the lawful presentation of the child. That is why the manuscripts vary; some have "the days of her purification" (Mary's), others "the days of his purification" (Jesus'). The Vulgate translates "eius," hence "his" (purification). But that is not too important; the sense is clear: Joseph and Mary wished to fulfill all the demands of the law. The sacrificial offerings were supposed to be larger than those described in Luke. The law prescribed that for the first born male child redemption money of five shekels was to be paid (Nm 18:15-18; cf. Nm 3:47; Ex 13:13-15), and further stipulated that a year old lamb as a burnt offering, and a young dove or a turtle dove as an offer of atonement, were to be given for the purification. Or, if the sacrifice of a lamb was not possible, a young dove or a turtle dove for each of the two offerings.

Five shekels equal about a dollar and a half in today's money. The Talmud treatise *Bekhoroth* says this payment was still customary in Jesus' time. Although Luke doesn't mention it, Joseph could have paid it. Of course it is also possible that Luke deliberately did not mention it, since, as Laurentin notes, "Levites" did not have to make this payment, because they belonged to the Lord.[1] If it is true that Jesus was not subject to the ceremony of redemption payment, then this would indicate a Levite form of offering, and this would strongly confirm his descent from a priestly tribe through his mother, Mary, who accordingly did not belong to the house of David, but a Levitican line (thus also Laurentin).

The attempt has often been made to infer from this kind of

1. R. Laurentin, *Structure et Théologie de Luc I–II*, 1957, p. 113 f.

offering the principal evidence for Joseph's alleged poverty. It
does state in Leviticus that two doves was the offering of the
poor. It is, however, very doubtful that this custom remained
unaltered for over 1500 years. The letter remains, but usage
changes. When once the law permitted the sacrifice of two doves,
this custom gradually spread more and more during the course
of the centuries. In Jesus' day it was no doubt only the really
"rich" people who sacrificed a yearling lamb on such an occasion.
The "common folk" did not do it. If Joseph had done it anyway,
that would have caused a stir, and that was not his way. He stood
in awe of God and the service of God, and what law and custom
decently required he would do; but he would not do anything to
attract attention, especially since people might harbor the notion
he was parading haughtily because of Jesus' birth. No, he simply
brought the usual sacrifice of people of his class.

Would he have been too poor anyway, to have offered a year
old lamb? The price of such an animal was listed then at about
two and a half shekels. Even if he were poor, with the help of
his friends and relatives (and the gold of the magi) Joseph could
have obtained that amount, and could have bought the lamb;
and if this were the custom, he certainly would have done so.
It is rather clear that he did *not* intend a departure from custom.
Luke does not mention the size of the offering to stress the
"poverty" of Joseph; on the contrary, he wants to bring out how
carefully Joseph obeyed the law, and the notions of "poor"
and "rich" are far from his mind here. Besides, we pointed out
before several other reasons why Joseph would not be poor in the
usual sense of the word. Up to now these offerings have been
advanced as air-tight proof of Joseph's poverty, but in view of
the above, they hardly form even a cogent argument.

> And behold, there was in Jerusalem a man named Simeon,
> and this man was just and devout, looking for the consolation
> of Israel, and the Holy Spirit was upon him. And it had been

revealed to him by the Holy Spirit that he should not see death
before he had seen the Christ of the Lord. And he came by
inspiration of the Spirit into the temple. And when his parents
brought in the child Jesus, to do for him according to the custom
of the Law, he also received him into his arms and blessed God,
saying, "Now thou dost dismiss thy servant, O Lord, according
to thy word, in peace; Because my eyes have seen thy salvation,
which thou hast prepared before the face of all peoples: A light
of revelation to the Gentiles, and a glory for thy people Israel."
And his father and mother were marvelling at the things spoken
concerning him. And Simeon blessed them, and said to Mary
his mother, "Behold, this child is destined for the fall and for the
rise of many in Israel, and for a sign that shall be contradicted.
And thy own soul a sword shall pierce, that the thoughts of
many hearts may be revealed."

Luke 2:25–35

The presentation of Jesus in the temple takes on an extraordinarily solemn character with the advent of Simeon. Like the
shepherds, this Simeon is an otherwise unknown, quiet, truly
God-fearing man whom we meet here and know nothing else
about. The early church made him out to be the father of
Gamaliel (Acts 5:34 f.), though there are no real reasons given
for this. It is evident from Simeon—and the shepherds—that
fortunately there were also many devout Jews living in Israel.
In the temple there were several people like Simeon (and Anna);
the scribes and the Pharisees felt more at home in the synagogue.
When later under the leadership of the Lord's brother James, the
head of the Christian community in Jerusalem, a successful
mission to the Jews spread over all of Palestine and Arabia as far
as Asia Minor and Egypt, and converted many Jews and established many churches, then we can see the beginnings of all that
in those first incidents surrounding the birth of Christ.

Simeon's song of praise *Nunc dimittis*, "now lettest thou . . ."
is famous. The *Benedictus*, the *Magnificat*, and now here the *Nunc
dimittis* blend into the great *Gloria in excelsis* of the angels, and

so sound that very joy which is the keynote of all of Christmas.
Nunc dimittis . . .—from these words we rightly infer that Simeon
is an old man. The old Israelite gives joyful witness that he now
knows that God's promises have become reality, because he has
seen the salvation of God, his light, and his glory incarnate in
the new-born Messias.

Joseph and Mary wondered at this. Here a stranger had come
to them, taken the child in his arms, and begun a song of praise.
How did he know what to say? Were they living in such a
miraculous world, that everyone was apprised of the great
tidings that had befallen them?

Of course, if the shepherds of Bethlehem were guardians of
the temple flocks and so visited the temple regularly, pious folk
like Simeon and Anna would surely be acquainted with them.
That Simeon came to the temple at the inspiration of the Holy
Spirit, as Luke says, does not preclude the shepherds' having
told Simeon and Anna the news already known throughout
Judea (Lk 1:65), and so prompting the old man to go and see
the child in the temple on the fortieth day. He must have had
some knowledge of the events of the holy night, but the Spirit
made him also a witness of the faith, a prophet, who delivered
in inspired words what he was given to know and see.

At the same time, however, his words contained the first
prophecy of future sorrows. Notice that Simeon turned
deliberately to Mary. Her soul would be pierced by a sword—
the fall and rising again of many—a sign which shall be spoken
against! In what way this prophecy would be fulfilled, Simeon
did not say, nor did Joseph and Mary know. But the *Stabat
mater dolorosa* can be faintly heard here.

"We must not immediately conclude as we perhaps involuntarily might do, that Simeon's words are fulfilled in the figure
of Mary beneath the cross . . . Nor must we assume that Luke
is thinking of the fulfillment in this way, for he is not describing

the scene of Mary beneath the cross . . . Later and present day interpretation has it that the sword in Old Testament writings was a symbol of enmity (Ps 9:7; 16:13; 56:5), or also of destruction (2 S 12:10). The meaning in Luke 2:34 is: The Messias will be spoken against in Israel; he will meet with hostility. Thus the words and the symbol of the sword refer to the pain which Mary will feel when she sees the Christ encounter disbelief and enmity, and suffers these along with him."[2]

Although Simeon addressed his words to Mary, doubtless Joseph too would suffer because of the hostility and lack of faith that Jesus would encounter, although of course he would no longer be living when Jesus began his public preaching. But Simeon surely was not thinking of that when he addressed only Mary, nor is it likely that by so doing he meant that a woman and a mother would suffer more than a man. In Simeon's words lies an allusion to the universal motherhood of the one "full of grace."

"But Mary did not turn away from the piercing sword, but accepted it as a blessing. Simeon blessed both Mary and Joseph with the future sorrows of the child. They now received this blessing for the first time, and with the sorrows of Christ it became the blessing of the world Church."[3]

This very Joseph, who as a father bore a great responsibility, and who was concerned at every step for the welfare of the mother and child, listened to the words of sword and sorrow with a troubled heart. Yes, he would present Jesus in the temple— in obedience toward God's law, but he did it not without fear and trembling for Mary and Jesus.

After Luke tells of Simeon, his words of praise, and the prophecy in them of sorrows to come, he continues:

2. Schelkle, p. 79 f.

3. J. Weiger, *Mary, Mother of Faith* (Chicago, Regnery, 1958), and by the same author, *Maria von Nazareth*, 1954 (for Lk 2:25–35).

And there was Anna, a prophetess, daughter of Phanuel, of the tribe of Aser. She was of a great age, having lived with her husband seven years from her maidenhood, and by herself as a widow to eighty-four years. She never left the temple, worshipping with fastings and prayers night and day. And coming up at that very hour, she began to give praise to the Lord, and spoke of him to all who were awaiting the redemption of Jerusalem.

Luke 2:36–38

Anna, too, was old in years. From the fact that her lineage could be named (unusual at that time) it is reasonable to conclude that she stemmed from an esteemed family. The almost official designation "prophetess" indicates that Anna was a respected person in the temple—a woman, who as prophetess would be first to speak and be highly regarded because of her piety. That she "departed not from the temple" does not mean that she stayed there also at night—although the ancients understood it that way[4]—but rather that she was to be found there every day, and as a devout woman was generally honored not only because of her words but also her praying and fasting, and especially honored, naturally, by those awaiting the salvation of Israel. Along with this it becomes clear from the context what the prophetess was prophesying: The salvation of Israel was her theme, and likewise the joy of her listeners.

This woman added her words to those of Simeon, whom she had probably listened to, that she might also praise her Lord. Whether she added still further to the words of Simeon is not reported; a canticle of praise from Anna is lacking. But what she did say was meaningful: She, the prophetess, spoke of Jesus to all who were awaiting the salvation of Israel.

After the circumcision of Jesus in the temple of Jerusalem the Holy Family returned to Bethlehem. True, Luke speaks in the very next verse (2:39) of Nazareth and thus omits the flight to

4. According to M. J. Lagrange, p. 91.

Egypt; yet a stay in Bethlehem doubtless preceded the journey
to Nazareth.

We can imagine what grave considerations occupied Joseph.
In the entire hill country of Judea and now also in the temple,
people's attention had been attracted. Had Joseph also heard in
Jerusalem of the wise men's visit and of the synod of the scribes
with Herod? The visit of the magi had been only one or two
weeks earlier, and Joseph doubtless informed himself of any news
in Jerusalem. Anyone in his position might have done the same,
given the same responsibility. Herod had probably also learned—
or would find out any day—that the magi had not returned.
This would anger the vain king, and anger with him meant
danger. He would also hear that the wise men's "king" had
already been in the temple and would learn of the events there—
news that could only increase his anger . . . With such thoughts
in mind, Joseph went back to Bethlehem with Mary and the child.

> But when they had departed, behold, an angel of the Lord
> appeared in a dream to Joseph, saying, "Arise, and take the child
> and his mother, and flee into Egypt, and remain there until I
> tell thee. For Herod will seek the child to destroy him." So he
> arose, and took the child and his mother by night, and withdrew
> into Egypt, and remained there until the death of Herod; . . .
>
> Matthew 2:13–15[5]

It is quite clear why Joseph arose in the night and fled with
mother and child. He did not hesitate one minute after the decision

5. It is remarkable that the gospel of Luke, intended for the pagan world,
describes what took place in the Jewish temple, the meeting with Simeon and
Anna, but it does not contain the story of the wise men, which is the very thing
one would look for in a gospel for the Gentiles. And Matthew, who is writing
primarily for the Hebrews, relates the visit of the wise men and the circumstances
leading to the flight to Egypt, but doesn't mention the events in the temple, so
important to Jewish minds. One often encounters such contrasts in the gospels,
contrasts which bear out what we read in the second epistle of Peter: "For we
were not following fictitious tales when we made known to you the power and
coming of our Lord Jesus Christ . . ." (2 Pt 1:16).

was made. "Arise," said the angel; it was then night, and he dared not wait till daybreak. His obedience to the word of the angel was all the more prompt now that he knew he could at last escape the dangers that haunted him day and night. Had it not been for his firm resolve earlier to wait out the time until he could visit the temple with Mary and the child, he would have left Bethlehem long before this. Learning now of the immediate danger, he did not hesitate to leave.

The journey through the desert to Egypt lasted somewhat longer than a week, and of course for the mother and child a mule was necessary on the journey. That such an animal was available in the middle of the night leads us to suppose that he had kept it with him since his departure from Nazareth, so that it was now of use to him again. Perhaps he even had two mules, for there must have been quite a number of things to take along. At any rate he was ready for the trip whether or not he had planned for the return to Nazareth. In itself the journey was not without danger, for the bands of Judas of Galilee made the desert between Israel and Egypt unsafe for travel. But refugees from Herod's kingdom would not receive bad treatment at their hands.

The flight to Egypt began towards fall, still ahead of the rainy season in the year 7 B.C., and the Holy Family remained there until after the death of Herod about the beginning of April of the year 4 B.C. Their stay in Egypt must have lasted therefore about three years. Hippolytus[6] says that Jesus remained three years and seven months in Egypt.[7]

6. Commentary on Daniel 12:1 and Matthew 24:22 in: *Hippolytus' Werke, Exegetische und homiletische Schriften*, ed. by G. N. Bonwetsch and H. Achelin, 1897.

7. Moreover, if we subtract a few months from these three years and seven months, namely the time it takes for the Holy Family to receive the news of Herod's death and to get ready for their return journey, then we arrive also in this way at the year 7 B.C. as Jesus' birth year.

We do not know if Herod struck right away, but it is a safe guess that he did, for the angel urged haste in his warning to Joseph. The flight was probably just at the right time. Although the king may not have received word immediately that the wise men had departed for home without returning to him, he learned soon enough. Perhaps the king also heard how great was the enthusiasm of the many visitors to the temple who heard Simeon's and Anna's words. All of this would have been more than enough to goad the irascible Herod to action. He dispatched his band of assassins.

He had already found out from the wise men how old the child might be. The planetary conjunction ran its course in three stages; the child could have been born even during the first stage and three-fourths of a year had elapsed since then. In short, the king ordered all boys of two years old and under to be killed. He did not make the age bracket too narrow; it mattered little to him whether a few boys more or less were killed. "All male children of two years and under in Bethlehem and vicinity are to be killed," was the way his order read. And the order was carried out.

Soon Bethlehem saw itself surrounded, and the soldiers killed the infants as they were commanded. The number is differently reported; some say from thirteen to fifteen children, others say from twenty to thirty. We consider the latter number more probable; the locale was indeed small, but the "entire vicinity" would not have been reckoned as small by soldiers who well knew how the king wanted his commands to be carried out.

> Then was fulfilled what was spoken through Jeremias the prophet, saying, "A voice was heard in Rama, weeping and loud lamentation; Rachel weeping for her children, and she would not be comforted, because they are no more."
>
> Matthew 2:17–18; cf. Jeremiah 31:15

Thus the events of Christmas in Bethlehem come to an end with blood and tears; the joy over all the things the shepherds and the magi experienced and told about ends in deep pain. And so the Messias enters the shadow of the cross even as he comes into the world.

They knew in Bethlehem that at least the little boy Jesus did not fall victim to Herod's blood bath. Perhaps people even told the soldiers that he had escaped, just to save their own children. Yet orders were orders, especially with Herod, and the fact that the child they were seeking had escaped, as people had said, would have been carefully concealed by the soldiers to save their own necks, or possibly to avoid being sent out to search further in the dangerous deserts to the south. They rendered their report: What we were ordered to do has been done; no one can have escaped in Bethlehem and its surroundings.

The murdered children were the first martyrs for Jesus, the *flores martyrum*, ("flowers of the martyrs") as Prudentius calls them. [8]

Matthew recalls in his gospel (2:18) an event that took place in 587 B.C. The Babylonian general Nabuzaradan had gathered many prisoners, among them Jeremiah, in Rama, about two hours' journey on foot to the north of Jerusalem, in order to lead them into exile. Jeremiah thought of Rachel, who lay buried in Bethlehem (Gen 35:19), and how, long ago, she had wept because of her abducted children. Of itself this incident has no direct bearing on Bethlehem, nor did Rachel lie buried in Rama, as a later tradition has it. Matthew was aware of all this; he mentions Rama purposely because of the grief over the lost children.

Flavius Josephus makes no mention of the slaughter in

8. If Jesus was born at the end of August, the massacre of the innocents therefore took place in October, and accordingly the liturgical day for this would actually have to be fixed also for October.

Bethlehem, at least not directly. As horrible as this deed was, there were many such deeds in Herod's realm, and from the standpoint of world history, the killing in Bethlehem was a small event in a kingdom where the entire Hasmonaean royal family, the queen, and all the successors to the throne had been assassinated. Perhaps Flavius Josephus had the children's murder in mind when he mentions that toward the end of his reign Herod raged with frightful cruelty "against guilty and innocent alike."

But we must not forget that Flavius Josephus was not and dared not be impartial. In the destruction of Jerusalem in 70 A.D., he said that the Emperor Vespasian was the Messias looked for by the Jews, a move which not only saved his own life, but obtained for him a tax-free estate and the imperial favor. Because of this he no doubt felt constrained to mention Christianity as little as possible, and to put what was absolutely necessary to say about it in an unfavorable light. The result was that after the triumph of Christianity in the West, many passages concerning Jesus in Flavius' manuscripts were deleted; the unfavorable and consciously partisan statements were not tolerated in the west. But in the East manuscripts were preserved in which those passages were retained.

Adolf von Harnack could say in 1900 that we "could write down the extra-evangelic statements concerning Jesus on one *quarto-size page*," but today one can find about *seven printed pages* of words about Jesus in the sixteen preserved old Russian manuscripts of Flavius' work. This was pointed out even in the nineteenth century by the Russians Andrei N. Popov (1866) and Ismail Sreznievski (1879). Their arguments went unheeded. The Baltic scholar Alexander Berendts (d. 1912) devoted thorough investigation to the question. We now have the results of all this in the work of R. Eisler, *Jesous basileus ou basileusas*, 2 vols., 1929–1930.[9]

In this significant work the passages in Flavius' work that were deleted in the west clearly show that Josephus and his age knew considerably more of Jesus than is found in our editions of Josephus. To be sure, those deleted passages had a negative content, but much can be inferred from that negative element that substantiates the familiar dates affirmed by us. It would lead us too far afield here to follow this path to new conclusions, nor is it necessary. However, an important fund of information is now available for scholarly investigation.

9. The title is taken from the Russian Josephus-manuscripts; according to these this "title" was above the temple portals of "Gate of Jesus the Crucified"; it means: "Jesus the king, who did not rule as king." The Jews wrote that because Pilate (Jn 19:21) refused to let them write in place of "King of the Jews," the inscription "He said, I am the King of the Jews"; a kind of small, belated revenge for the Jews.

CHAPTER VI

EGYPT

THE HOLY FAMILY remained in Egypt for over three years. Our calculation agrees with the period of three to three and a half years handed down by tradition. Hippolytus, whom we mentioned earlier, points out that this period of time is alluded to in the Revelation of St. John (12:13 f.): "And when the dragon saw that he was cast unto the earth, he persecuted the woman which brought forth the man child. And to the woman were given two wings of a great eagle, that she might fly into the wilderness, into her place, where she is nourished for a time and (two) times, and half a time, from the face of the serpent." To be sure, John is speaking here as the writer of the Apocalypse, and does not intend to specify the length of time, so that three and a half "times" corresponds only approximately to three and a half years. Hippolytus calculates three years and seven months. Mary, however, lived many years in the home of John,[1] and so he was especially familiar with the life of the holy virgin. It is obvious that he based his apocalyptic vision on the account of the flight of Mary to Egypt, and is recalling that this period embraced

1. John went to Ephesus when the threatening war made staying in Palestine too dangerous for Mary. It is possible that Mary concluded her earthly life in Jerusalem, before John went to Ephesus (the Jerusalem-tradition); it is also possible that Mary went with John to Ephesus (the Ephesus-tradition); in any case we may assume she lived in Jerusalem until John's departure from that city.

three and a half years. The early Church understood this to be the case, and in our opinion, with complete justification.

Matthew cites the second part of the prophecy of Hosea (11:1): "When Israel was a child, then I loved him, *and called my son out of Egypt.*" Every Israelite could understand that the son of God that Hosea referred to was the people of Israel, which God called his "first-born son" (Ex 4:22; Jer 31:9) after their liberation from Egypt. The flight of the Messias to that very country, Egypt, was ordained by God and his will in this made known to Joseph so that in the close similarity between the history of Jesus' early youth and the early history of the Jewish nation the Jews might recognize Jesus as the Messias.

Just where Joseph turned to in Egypt is fairly certain right from the start. The gospels, which of course had as their purpose the announcement of the kingdom of God and not the writing of exact history, do not report anything further of the stay of the Holy Family in Egypt. Yet this sojourn must have been very important. It is usually too little noted that in Egypt at that time there was a Jewish community in exile which equalled in number the Jewish population of Palestine. In Palestine at that time there were approximately one million Jews. Among the 7,800,000 inhabitants of Egypt there were likewise one million Jews, who enjoyed in that country a freedom and status undreamed of in Palestine. In the third century B.C. the famous Septuagint, the Greek translation of the Old Testament, was made there. In the second and first centuries B.C., during and after the wars in which the Maccabeans achieved fame, countless Jews emigrated to Egypt. In Alexandria, trade was mostly in the hands of Jews, and the wealth of the Alexandrian Jews was proverbial.

There was a great difference between Judaism in the east (Babylon, etc.) and Judaism in the west (Egypt, Italy, Greece, Asia Minor). The former was Judaistic, the latter, Hellenistic, and Judaism in Egypt formed the nucleus of the Judeo-Hellenistic movement. Not only because the Septuagint was written here, but also because of the great Jewish philosopher Philo (born 20 B.C.), who was the author and leader of the Hellenistic movement, and who lived in Alexandria when the Holy Family was in Egypt. In the first century B.C., Alexandria was the greatest city of the Roman Empire, next to Rome itself. The library in Alexandria was the largest and most famous of all the libraries in antiquity. It was for the most part destroyed in 391 A.D., and the remainder lost when the Arabs under Omar conquered Alexandria in 641. But at the time Joseph was in Egypt (and even later, when Peter preached here), it was in its flower. It is hard to overstate the life of the Jews in Egypt; they enjoyed at least the same standards as the Palestinian Jews.[2]

The point of dispute between the Jews of Palestine and those of Egypt was the temple. When in Palestine under the Syrians the high priest Onias III was assassinated, his son Onias sought refuge in Egypt. King Ptolemy not only received him in friendly fashion, but also put at his disposal an unused pagan temple in Leontopolis (Matanae, or Matare), that he might convert it into a Jewish sanctuary. This temple came into being through the riches of Alexandrian and other Egyptian Jews; it became large and magnificent, much larger and more magnificent than the temple of Zorobabel in Jerusalem. In 160 B.C. it was completed, and was justifiably considered to be the pride of all the Jews in Egypt, who had their own high priest and their religious center here.

Judaism in Israel felt itself to be more closely allied with eastern Judaism (to which the Israelites owed the Babylonian Talmud), and feared the Hellenistic Judaism, which threatened to arrogate leadership to itself. But the real object of their concern was the temple at Leontopolis. Judaism per se could recognize no second

2. Cf. E. Schürer, *Geschichte des jüdischen Volkes*, 4th ed. 1901–1911; A. Edersheim, *Life and Times*, etc., 36th ed. 1953.

temple outside of the Jerusalemic one. It contradicted the Jewish conception of service in the temple to think of this service as divided in more than one place. The mere existence of the temple in Egypt, so the rabbis feared, meant an undermining of the essence of Jewish religion, a splintering of the one and only possible religious center in Jerusalem. God dwelt in the temple of Jerusalem, and only there. Israel had not been able to escape entirely the influence of Hellenism; the New Testament, with the exception of the Aramaic Matthew gospel, was, after all, written in Greek. But in principle, because of this temple, there was hostility toward Egyptian Hellenism. In the East they were content with synagogues; that in Egypt they were not, but rather elevated this temple to a new house of God, with a high priest and a regular temple service, and behaved very independently, was the occasion of considerable unrest.

Naturally it was very difficult for Judaism to solve the problem. The large Jewish population of Egypt could not simply be ordered to go to Jerusalem on the great feast days. There had to be tacit toleration of the fact that Egyptian Jews had a temple service of their own which resembled the one in Jerusalem. The Egyptian "heretics," however, were simply not mentioned in Jerusalem. In the schools of the scribes, in rabbinical literature, and in popular tradition one seldom finds mention of the Onias temple. It was an unwritten law in Israel to keep silent about it for the sake of the one and indivisible temple in Jerusalem. On the other hand, the Egyptian Jews, especially the ones in Alexandria, gave generous gifts to Jerusalem and the temple there; even the Herodian temple, which excelled the Onias temple in splendor, received very valuable and precious gifts, visible to everyone, for instance the great bronze doors. The Jews in Jerusalem accepted these gifts "silently"; the gifts to them were more or less regarded as a penance offering, and in any case considered to be a tribute that was owed them. The Alexandrians bore this with a quiet smile; they wanted no enmity, and certainly no theological enmity, which is the worst kind.

The early Christian Church also could not quite refrain from this silent verdict. We know that Joseph went to Egypt, but we are told nothing of what he encountered or did there. In the gospels we read almost nothing concerning the life of the Jews in Egypt. Even the Acts of the Apostles is silent on this score; it shows us Asia Minor, Greece, and Italy, but the vast areas of apostolic work in distant Asia, and especially Egypt with its large Jewish population, are not mentioned at all. The Church in Egypt, with its important scholarly theological schools of the second century under Pantaenus, Clemens Alexandrinus, etc., must have had a good foundation even then. But Acts tells us nothing about it. After Peter departed from Palestine, according to the Acts of the Apostles, there was a period of six to eight years before he took up his work in Italy. Where was he during all those years? It is reasonable to suppose he was in Egypt. Acts makes no mention of it, although because of Peter important things must have taken place there. Indeed, the Church in Alexandria was the largest in Christendom, larger than the Church in Antioch, or Rome, or anywhere else in Europe or Asia. This might be very plausibly explained by tracing it back to the activities there of the prince of the apostles.

Just where did Joseph go? Tradition has it that he went to Matanae (or Matare), and so to Leontopolis, with its great Jewish temple! And what we know of Joseph fits this assumption very well. If he, like his ancestors, was a refugee from the land of Israel and could now no longer visit the temple in Jerusalem, where else would he turn but to the temple in the land affording him asylum? After all he had experienced in Nazareth and Bethlehem, it was natural for Joseph to seek out the center of religious life in Egypt. Would he not even consider this as his sacred duty? After all, it was his responsibility to make the way smooth for the newborn king of the Jews! Tradition gives the obvious and the correct explanation. In Leontopolis not only a refuge awaited him, but a task as well.

Would Joseph and Mary have kept silent here concerning the miraculous events of Christmas? Was that their duty? By no means! They naturally had the responsibility of carefully shielding the child from any who were seeking to take his life, but silence was definitely not their assignment. When the angels proclaimed the glad tidings to be shared by the whole world, then shepherds, and elders and everyone who heard it and knew it were entrusted with the happy work of spreading this news, and insofar as they were able, to acquaint the whole world with it. To be silent would have been inconceivably faint-hearted and neglectful, qualities we cannot impute to Joseph and Mary.

They were at that time not the only fugitives from Herod's realm. Conditions in that kingdom gave rise to a continuous stream of people fleeing from there. The Jewish rebels obtained provisions from their co-religionists in Egypt. Whatever occurred in Bethlehem would soon have become known in Egypt, and what people now heard from Joseph and Mary in person was only a confirmation of what they had heard previously. Or were people who awaited the consolation of Israel only to be found in Judea? Certainly not. We know of no Simeon and Anna in the temple of Onias, but that does not mean that there were not any such. On the contrary, many of the best of the Jews gathered in Egypt. Anyone who could not accommodate to conditions in the old country found here the opportunity for a new life in freedom. If we are looking for an explanation of the extraordinarily rapid growth of the Christian Church in Egypt, we find it first of all in the sojourn of the Holy Family in Egypt and in the Christmas tidings made known there through them. If we knew of nothing else but their three and a half year stay in Egypt, that would be enough to understand many things. When the great "fisherman" Peter cast his net here for several years, he could not haul it in because of the size of the catch. He built on a strong foundation, and so great churches arose. If the magnificent Serapeum with its costly library had not been sacked and burned (391 A.D.), who knows what historical treasures, now unhappily beyond our reach, might have enriched this chapter. As it is we must be content for the most part with inferences.

> But when Herod was dead, behold, an angel of the Lord appeared in a dream to Joseph in Egypt, saying, "Arise, and take the child and his mother, and go into the land of Israel, for those who sought the child's life are dead." So he arose and took the child and his mother, and went into the land of Israel. But hearing that Archelaus was reigning in Judea in place of his father Herod, he was afraid to go there; and being warned in a dream, he withdrew into the region of Galilee. And he went and settled in a town called Nazareth; that there might be fulfilled what was spoken through the prophets, "He shall be called a Nazarene."
>
> Matthew 2:19–23; cf. Isaiah 4:2; 11:1

Herod the Great died in April of the year 4 B.C.; he was buried in the castle Herodium in the vicinity of Bethlehem! Herod had ten wives altogether. The first, Doris, bore him his oldest and worst son, Antipater. The Maccabean princess Mariamne had two sons, Alexander and Aristobulus, who were murdered by their father; another Mariamne gave him a son, Herod Philippus; Malthake, a Samaritan, bore him Archelaus and Herod Antipas; and the Jerusalemic Cleopatra was the mother of Philippus. Antipater, Alexander, and Aristobulus were already dead, Herod Philippus inherited riches, but not the right to rule (he lived in Jerusalem), and the three remaining sons, Archelaus, Herod Antipas, and Philippus succeeded him as rulers. The first received the title Ethnarch ("tribal prince"), the last two had to be satisfied with the title Tetrarch ("the ruler of a fourth part"). Archelaus ruled over Judea, Herod Antipas, Galilee and Perea; he became the governor of the region in which Jesus grew up. Philippus received a few northern regions.

Antipater, Herod's eldest son and already dead, was regarded as the worst one, but Archelaus ran him a close second. He began his reign with a blood bath that reached to the very court yards of the temple, and cost the lives of three thousand people; he was just as cruel as his father Herod, but possessed neither his talent nor his energy, and in the year 6 A.D. was banished to Gaul by the emperor because of his enormities. After him, Roman prefects came to Judea.

It is striking that the angel says to Joseph: "for *they are* dead which sought the young child's life." In itself this might have indicated the enmity of many, but from the historical context it is clear that Herod and his son Antipater are meant. This Antipater was the evil spirit of the Herod before him. Flavius Josephus points to Antipater as the instigator of the assassination of Mariamne's sons, and characterizes him as ready to murder anyone who might dispute his claim to the throne after his father's death. Flavius further describes him as Herod's advisor and unofficial regent, who in his father's last years practically controlled the throne (*Ant.* 16, 17).

When Herod finally fell ill, and the illness of the father lasted "too long" for the son, Antipater organized a conspiracy against his father. However, he did not proceed cleverly enough, for Herod discovered the conspiracy and did not deprive himself of the pleasure of later having his son strangled five days before his own death. Thus, both Herod and Antipater died almost at the same time, and it was no doubt to this that the angel had reference.

Also in earlier times the meaning of these circumstances was alluded to. In Patrizi (*De Evangeliis*, III, p. 377), we find an old exegesis of Matthew, in which there is the statement, attributed to St. Athanasius: "But they who sought to kill Jesus were Herod the king, and Antipater, his son."

If this interpretation is right—and it would seem to be—then new approaches are given for the dating of the birth of Jesus and the events in Bethlehem. According to the detailed account of Flavius Josephus, apparently Antipater was no longer the regent of the king in the last year before the latter's death. He stayed in Rome for seven months, was taken into custody on his return and imprisoned for several months before his death by strangulation. The time at which Antipater together with his father sought the death of Jesus must have been at least a year and a half before Herod's death. Also, Antipater did not attain to any power until after the death of his brothers Alexander and Aristobulus. Thus the period of time for the birth of Jesus and the events in Bethlehem is restricted to the years 747 and 748 A.U.C. This agrees with everything that we have already established.

On the basis of the text we may assume that Joseph considered the possibility of staying at Bethlehem on his return from Egypt. More than three years had elapsed since he had left Nazareth, and after so long an absence he may not have thought his work in Nazareth so important any more. Possibly he also now considered Bethlehem, the city of David, the most suitable residence because of his son. However, on the way there he heard disturbing reports that made it clear to him he should avoid Judea. And so he returned to Nazareth.

The supposition that he had left one or more of his sons by the first marriage in charge of his workshop in Nazareth gains credence by the fact that he was now able to take up his work again there or possibly work with his sons. Later, when Joseph had died, the gospel speaks of "the mother and brothers" in Nazareth. In this context, our interpretation and also the oldest tradition of the Church is again confirmed that Joseph was an elderly man with several children from a previous marriage.

Matthew does not know, it would seem, that Joseph and Mary had earlier lived in Nazareth. He writes as if they were going to Nazareth for the first time: "And he [Joseph] came and dwelt in a city called Nazareth." But it can also be reasonably maintained that with these words Matthew leaves the possibility open that Joseph, after receiving the warning in a dream to go to Galilee, automatically chose Nazareth simply because he had lived there before—a fact which Matthew would naturally know.

In Luke there is another striking "gap": When Joseph, Mary, and Jesus had encountered Simeon and Anna in the temple, he writes: "And when they had performed all things [in the temple] according to the law of the Lord, they returned into Galilee, to their own city Nazareth." Many are of the opinion that Luke seems not to know that at least three years in Egypt lay between the temple visit and the arrival in Nazareth. Yet there is no need to see a contradiction here, for neither account invalidates the other by any means.

Nor is it necessary to "harmonize" them, for omniscience is an attribute of God, not of men. Furthermore, we must remember that the evangelists had no intention of writing a biography of Jesus, but wanted rather to report the Good News. Finally, it must be kept in mind that the evangelists did not write down everything they knew; to each one of them we can apply the saying of John at the end of his gospel: "And there are also many other things which Jesus did, the which, if they should be written every one, I suppose that even the world itself could not contain the books that should be written."

Although born in Bethlehem, Jesus was afterwards called a Nazarene (Mt 2:23; 26:71; Mk 1:24; 10:47; 14:67; 16:6; Lk 4:34). Once in the New Testament Christians are also called Nazarenes (Acts 24:5), and the Mohammedans use this designation even

today (*nasrani*). As we know from John 1:45 f., the names
Nazareth and Nazarene could have at that time a pejorative
meaning: "Philip findeth Nathanael [from Cana] and saith unto
him, we have found him, of whom Moses in the law, and the
prophets, did write, Jesus of Nazareth, the son of Joseph. And
Nathanael said unto him, 'Can there any good thing come out
of Nazareth?' "

It is not clear whether Nathanael is alluding to an unpleasant
personal experience with one or more Nazarenes, or whether
Nathanael's town Cana and Nazareth were not on good terms,
or whether Nazareth itself had a bad reputation. The last is
unlikely; according to historical evidence Nazareth was not in
bad repute. Yet Nathanael's remark set a pattern for the later
use of Nazarene as a term of insult.

Although a center of trade, Nazareth was a small village,
and the scornful use of the name probably meant that a prophet
or a "sect" coming from such a hick town could not possibly
amount to anything. Also, Galilee was not highly regarded anyway
among the Jews of the south because of its mixed population,
and it didn't even have a representative metropolis near it.
Nazareth was in this *galiel ha-gojim* ("land of heathens") only a
small and insignificant village.

What is harder to understand is what Matthew means when
he says ". . . that it might be fulfilled which was spoken by the
prophets, He shall be called a Nazarene." For nowhere in the
Old Testament is there anything that says Jesus would come from
Nazareth or be called a Nazarene. And Matthew knew this as
well as we do. But since he nevertheless mentions this, then there
is either a play on words or a commonly understood notion
behind his statement, perhaps even both.

The pun available to Matthew, the Hebrew, comes about
when we reduce the word Nazareth to its root *nezer* and then
re-read the prophecy in Isaiah 11:1 that a sprout, or offshoot

(*nezer*) will break forth from the stem of Jesse. Matthew is saying: The Nazarene, the *nezer* or branch of Jesse's tribe, is insulted with this name, as if the great Messias could not come from such a lowly place as Nazareth; yet Isaiah, the great prophet, has foretold just that by his use of the word!

Such a play on words would be obvious to Matthew, for the rabbinical literature, with which he was familiar, had worked out this "branch-theme" especially in connection with Isaiah 11:1 (cf. Jer 23:5; 35:15). This literature knew eight names for the awaited Messias, and the most important of these was *semach* ("offshoot, branch")—i.e., *nezer*. Even the fifteenth eulogy of the daily liturgy in the temple repeated this thought every day in its free rendition of the Isaiah prophecy (cf. the Talmud treatise *Berakhoth*). The Jewish readers—and Matthew wrote for them —therefore understood immediately this play on words; it was familiar enough to them. But to them (as to Matthew) it was much more; it was the fulfillment of a prophecy.

Along with this a more general thought may have played a part: The prophets spoke again and again of how lowly, how despised and rejected the Messias would be among his own people; the rabbis had hitherto involuntarily emphasized this point in their interpretations of the above mentioned *nezer*-prophecy. Now Matthew was saying to them and to his people: See how this *nezer*-prophecy foretold how the Messias would be; this prophecy fits Jesus, he is the branch from David's stem!

CHAPTER VII

THE FEAST OF CHRISTMAS

IN THE course of our exposition it has become clear that the celebration of Christmas in December is not historically well founded. We have shown that the visit of the wise men took place at the end of September, the visit to the temple (on the fortieth day after the birth) in the first week of October, and accordingly, the birth of Jesus at the end of August. We do not know the exact date, of course.

It is worthy of note that the earliest Church knew no feast of Jesus' birth. The death on the cross and the resurrection occupied the center of their interest, and since there was concern about other things in setting forth matters of faith and doctrine, there was no necessity for examining the reliability of the traditional birth date of Jesus. Of course there were individual attempts at an exact dating. Thus in the third century Clement of Alexandria spoke of the nineteenth of April; others said the twenty-ninth of May, or the twenty-eighth of March; still others maintained that Jesus had been born in the summer, but gave various dates for this. By and large, too little importance was attached to the question for people to have seriously concerned themselves with it.

The situation began to change during the Arian controversies in the fourth century. The Alexandrian presbyter Arius (d. 336) and his adherents taught that Jesus Christ was not God's son in the true and proper sense of the word. The struggle with the Arian sect led to a further development of Christology, and the Council of Nicaea (325) finally set forth a creed which stated: Jesus Christ is the true son of God and of the same nature as the Father. After the condemnation of Arianism at this council, there was formed in opposition to the declining Arian sect a "catholic" cult, whose concern was the establishment of a feast day for the birth of Jesus Christ. Proceeding from Rome as a center, it attempted to overcome Arianism not only in theory—this had been done at the council—but also in a practical way.

Arianism vanished quickly in southern Europe. Also in the west, through the efforts of the Emperor Valentinian II (375–392), it was soon overcome. But among the Germanic tribes it was prevalent for a long time. This was not because they necessarily agreed with Arius in his Christology, but because he had recommended that the church service be held in the vernacular. In the great battles of the folk migrations, however, Rome was very much interested in rooting out Arianism among these advancing Germanic tribes. In this struggle the "catholic" feast of Christmas became an outright symbol.

In this situation Rome did something else of great significance. The pagan Teutons (paganism had not fully died out even among the Teutons who were Arian Christians) celebrated their yule feast in January and the festival of the fires on December twenty-fifth. This was on the basis of the Julian calendar, in which the winter solstice fell on December twenty-fifth (this was later changed to December twenty-first in the Gregorian calendar). Rome now decreed the feast of the Nativity to be held on the twenty-fifth of December, and said that on this day the yule festival was truly celebrated (yule means "joy"). The catholic custom was sustained. The Langobards were the last ones (662) to become "catholic." And since that time the twenty-fifth of December has been the feast day of the Nativity. As the almanac of Filozalus tells us, it is supposed to have been celebrated in Rome for the first time on December twenty-fifth in the year 354; there is, however, also a report of a celebration of the Nativity on December twenty-fifth, in the year 336.

When in the sixteenth century the Gregorian calendar changed the date of the winter solstice from December twenty-fifth (of the Julian calendar) to December twenty-first, the date of the Nativity feast should actually have been changed, too. The church stayed by the December twenty-fifth date, and she did so for an important reason. January first was of course universally celebrated as New Year's Day and took the form of a secular festival. The fixing of the feast of the Nativity on December twenty-fifth made it possible to consecrate January first as the feast day of the Circumcision of Jesus, for the circumcision had occurred on the eighth day after birth. And so the fitting thought came to mind that in place of the old Roman new year's day on March first, dedicated to the war god Mars, the new year would now begin with Jesus, the prince of peace. For this reason the church kept the December twenty-fifth date, even though the Gregorian calendar dated the winter solstice on December twenty-first.

Little by little the non-western churches followed the Roman custom. In the Greek world it had been formerly the practice to celebrate the feast of the Epiphany (epiphany means "appearance"); it was celebrated on January sixth, and had reference to the baptism of Jesus in the Jordan, whereby the actual epiphany of Jesus as God's son was discerned (for the Holy Spirit descended on Jesus and the voice of God said: "This is my beloved Son, in whom I am well pleased"). This feast was also celebrated as the feast of the nativity of Jesus. When later the Greek church celebrated the nativity of Jesus as a separate feast on December twenty-fifth, as in the western church, the feast of the Epiphany could no longer remain a nativity feast, but it did remain the feast of his baptism. Even today in the Greek church on Epiphany the consecration of the baptismal water takes place.

In the West, on the other hand, this feast of Epiphany was not known. But then later the eastern practice was adopted; it became associated with the arrival of the wise men from the East, and although the Greek name of the feast was not interpreted entirely accurately this way, the idea of the appearance of Christ to the pagan world (the magi) was an ingenious one. From the fifth to the eighth century this catholic mode of celebration was gradually adopted by the entire Church.

Of course, it would be nicer if the entire arrangement of this calendar of feasts accorded with the historical reality. That it does not was known in the early centuries just as well as we know it today. As we sketched above, there were other considerations which determined the cycle of feast days—doubtless good, practical, and fruitful considerations, but ones which unfortunately have attracted some of the pomp of the yule festival over to Christmas. But anyone who truly wants a right understanding of the history of Jesus' birth must spare no effort in examining these considerations and in penetrating to the real events. A realm of overpowering truth and beauty will then be revealed, a story which is at the same time completely human and yet beyond all measure divine.

INDEX

145